Northamptonshire, Cambridgeshire, Leicestershire & Rutland

NICK BURTON

COUNTRYSIDE BOOKS
NEWBURY BERKSHIRE

First published 2005
© Martin Hall, 2005

COUNTRYSIDE BOOKS
3 Catherine Road
Newbury, Berkshire

To view our complete range of books,
please visit us at
www. countrysidebooks co.uk

ISBN 1 85306 900 0

Dedicated to Nicola and James
And thanks to my mother and father

Photographs by the author

Designed by Peter Davies, Nautilus Design
Produced through MRM Associates Ltd., Reading
Typeset by Jean Cussons Typesetting, Diss, Norfolk
Printed by Arrowsmith, Bristol

Contents

Contents

WALKS IN LEICESTERSHIRE & RUTLAND

PUBLISHER'S NOTE

We hope that you obtain considerable enjoyment from this book; great care has been taken in its preparation. Although at the time of publication all routes followed public rights of way or permitted paths, diversion orders can be made and permissions withdrawn.

We cannot, of course, be held responsible for such diversion orders and any inaccuracies in the text which result from these or any other changes to the routes nor any damage which might result from walkers trespassing on private property. We are anxious, though, that all details covering the walks are kept up to date and would therefore welcome information from readers which would be relevant to future editions.

The simple sketch maps that accompany the walks in this book are based on notes made by the author whilst checking out the routes on the ground. They are designed to show you how to reach the start, to point out the main features of the overall circuit and they contain a progression of numbers that relate to the paragraphs of the text.

However, for the benefit of a proper map, we do recommend that you purchase the relevant Ordnance Survey sheet covering your walk. The Ordnance Survey maps are widely available, especially through booksellers and local newsagents.

Introduction

Walking in the countryside is becoming increasingly popular. It is an enjoyable way to keep fit and healthy, and is the perfect antidote to the stresses of modern living. What's more – it's completely free of charge! Of the 40 routes in this book, 39 are circular and 1 is linear. Each walk begins and ends at a recommended pub, where you will be able to enjoy a wide range of good food. All have been carefully designed to guide you through some of the most beautiful scenery in Northamptonshire, Cambridgeshire, Leicestershire & Rutland.

In Northamptonshire, you will find secluded river valleys, winding country roads and stone cottages topped with thatched roofs. In spring, woodland floors take on a splash of colour as bluebells and other wild flowers emerge from the ground to transform the pale hues of winter. A web of paths and tracks will lead you through meadows and over hills, beside tranquil canals and clear brooks. There are historic villages and fine stately homes to discover, and some fabulous views await you.

Cambridgeshire is best known for the fens, which dominate the flat landscape in central and northern parts of the county. This network of dykes and waterways has allowed flooding to be controlled, and has led to the creation of rich agricultural land. The first drainage was carried out by the Romans, but bigger and better systems were introduced by Dutch engineers during the 17th century. These scenic waterways also support an abundance of wildlife, which can be encountered on the walks. In contrast, the higher ground to the south offers sweeping views across the countryside. There are also rivers, ancient paths, pretty villages and country lanes to explore. The stunning cathedrals at Ely and Peterborough are well-known landmarks, while the city of Cambridge is, of course, famous for its historic university.

Leicestershire is a county of rolling terrain, dotted with woods and copses and crossed with some of the most beautiful stretches of waterways in England. Historic battles have been fought here and bustling market towns established long ago still thrive today. Walkers can discover hidden valleys and picture-postcard villages, long-distance paths and breathtaking views. Culinary history is unearthed on one of the routes, as you discover the birthplace of the famous Stilton cheese. Quaint traditions and the region's industrial heritage also reveal themselves along the way.

Rutland is well documented as being England's smallest county. It was recognised as an official Shire County in the 12th century, although its history goes back even further. It was an important centre of activity in Anglo-Saxon times, and many of the village names can be traced back to this period. In 1974, however, it was abolished under government reforms and merged with Leicestershire. Local people launched a long and vigorous campaign, and its county status was returned by popular demand in 1997. The walks in this book allow you to sample the impressive Rutland Water, undulating farmland, attractive hamlets and the peaceful countryside for which Rutland is renowned.

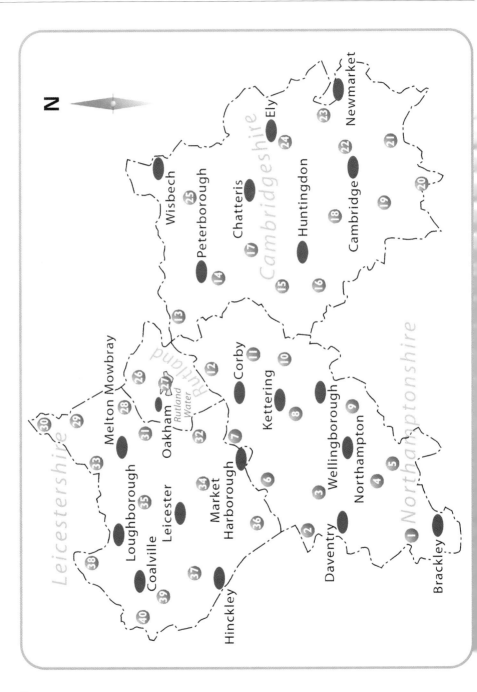

Near Donisthorpe, Leicestershire

Each of the routes is between 3 and 8 miles in length. Almost all of the featured pubs have a car park that you will be able to use, provided that you call in for refreshments. However, it is a good idea to ask the landlord for permission to leave your car before setting out on your walk. Roadside parking is available at those pubs without car parks. For those wishing to use public transport, a number of the walks are within reach of a railway station, or are accessible by bus. For details, call Traveline on 0870 6082608.

A sketch map is provided for each walk to help guide you along. However, I strongly recommend that you also carry with you the relevant Ordnance Survey map, as they are invaluable for highlighting detail. I have given the appropriate Explorer sheet number and title at the beginning of each route. A lightweight waterproof carried in a small rucksack will protect you from the changeable British weather, and you may wish to pack a drink and a snack, particularly on longer walks. A pair of walking boots is also recommended, especially on wet or muddy ground, and it's a good idea to change into clean footwear before entering the pub.

You will endear yourself to landowners if you leave gates as you find them and keep any dogs under control.

Finally, I hope that the routes in this book will bring you many happy hours of walking and encourage you to discover new places. Enjoy the countryside.

Martin Hall

Sulgrave
The Star Inn

a quiet rural location. The walk takes you beside streams and woodland, before leading you over higher ground, from where you can appreciate some fantastic views across the countryside.

The welcoming **Star Inn** dates back to the 16th century. In addition to the large single bar, which has a beamed ceiling, stone floors and, in winter, a roaring fire, there is a separate non-smoking dining room, and you will find a small beer garden

T he charming village of Sulgrave with its attractive stone houses, many with thatched roofs, enjoys at the rear of the building. A wide choice of food is served throughout, and examples from the regularly changing menu include deep-fried scallops with chilli dipping sauce, sausages and mash, and chickpea and aubergine fritters with an oregano and feta dressing. Regular ales are Hook Norton Best Bitter and Old Hooky. Various guest beers are also available.

Distance: *6½ miles*

OS Explorer 207 Newport Pagnell & Northampton South
GR 558455

A moderate walk on undulating ground

Starting point: The Star Inn's car park. Please ask the landlord before leaving your car whilst you walk.

How to get there: Sulgrave lies to the east of junction 11 of the M40 motorway. From the B4525, which runs between the A422 and the A43, follow signs to Sulgrave Manor. The pub is on Manor Road, close to the manor itself.

Opening times are 6 pm to 10 pm on Monday, 11 am to 2.30 pm and 6 pm to 11 pm on Tuesday to Saturday, and 12 noon to 5 pm on Sunday. Food is available at lunchtime from 12 noon to 2 pm (2.30 pm on Saturday and Sunday) and in the evening from 6.30 pm to 9 pm on Tuesday to Saturday. The pub is closed on Monday lunchtime and Sunday evening.

Telephone: 01295 760389.

The Walk

1 Leave the pub and turn left along the pavement. Pass Sulgrave Manor on your right and beautiful thatched houses on your left. Ignore a road off to the right, but keep straight ahead. Turn right along a signed bridleway, which curves to the left then the right. Cross a stream and go through an iron gate, then walk straight ahead to pass underneath an old railway bridge. Continue, keeping a hedge to your right. Further on, a pretty brook accompanies you to your right. The path curves to the left then the right, taking you across a stream. Walk straight on, with a hedge to your right. After 300 yards, you reach a marker post on your left.

2 Turn half-left here and cross a footbridge by a tree, then bear diagonally right. At the far side of the field, go through a gate and continue ahead. Bear left at the top of a slope and go over two stiles in quick succession. Continue with a wire fence to your left. Go over two more stiles in quick succession and walk ahead. At the end of a field, cross a stile and keep straight ahead. Go over another stile and pass farm buildings to your right. Continue straight on to a narrow lane.

3 Turn right along the lane and then right along a wider road. Turn right by the Crown Inn and walk up an incline, passing farm buildings on your right. Go over a stile on your left to follow a well-

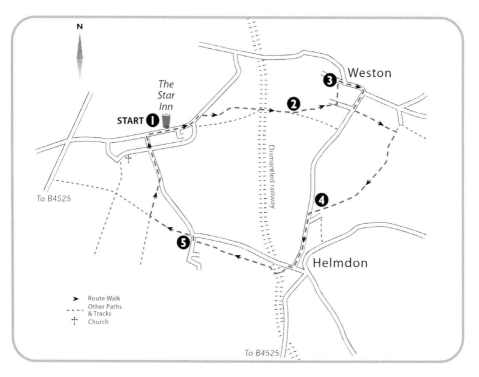

surfaced path, which curves to the right slightly, offering great views across the landscape. Turn right at a junction of paths further on and walk down a slope, keeping a hedge to your right. After 130 yards, a marker arrow on a post guides you diagonally left. At the far side of a field go through a gap in the hedge and turn right. Cross a footbridge over a stream and continue, keeping a hedge to your right. After about 400 yards, bear diagonally left across a field on an unmarked track. Go through a gap in the hedge and then turn half-left. At the corner of a field, go through a gap in the hedge and bear diagonally left. Walk across a field to a road.

Near Sulgrave at the start of the walk

4 Turn left and walk along the road with care. Continue uphill and then pass a timber yard on your right. Follow the road downhill and turn right at a T-junction. After passing a farm building, go over a stile on your left. Follow a signed path, keeping a hedge to your right. Walk ahead and then follow the path as it curves slightly right. Cross a dismantled railway line and turn right, keeping a line of trees to your right. After passing the line of a hedge on your left, bear diagonally left down a slope. Go over a stile and bear slightly right. At the far side of a field, go through a gap in the hedge and walk up an incline, with a hedge to your right. Where the hedge ends, bear round to the right and go through an iron gate on your right. Head diagonally left, aiming for a wooden fence. Go over two stiles in quick succession and continue ahead. Cross a stile in the corner of a field to arrive at a road junction.

5 Turn right then immediately left, along a signed footpath. Continue, with a hedge to your left. After about 750 yards, turn right by a kissing gate and cross a field, heading downhill. Go through a kissing gate and bear half-right. Go through another kissing gate and bear left, before crossing a footbridge to arrive at a road. Turn left along the road and walk up a gentle incline. Pass a road off to the right and continue ahead, then turn right along Manor Road to return to the Star Inn.

Date walk completed:

....

Places of Interest

Sulgrave Manor is situated about 200 yards north-east of the pub. This Tudor manor house and gardens was home to the ancestors of George Washington, the first President of the United States of America. Telephone: 01295 760205.

Canons Ashby House (National Trust) is located 3 miles north of Sulgrave. This Elizabethan manor house contains wall paintings and Jacobean plaster work. There is also a formal garden and the remains of an Augustinian priory. Telephone: 01327 861900.

The White Horse

engineering completed in 1797 and excavated using picks and shovels. Later, you walk through the pretty village of Ashby St Ledgers, which has connections to the failed Gunpowder Plot of 1605.

The White Horse is a lovely whitewashed building with a

This picturesque route begins in the village of Welton and leads you through an undulating landscape of fine views. The walk takes you beside the Grand Union Canal and along a path running parallel with Braunston Tunnel – a magnificent feat of thatched roof and floral hanging baskets outside. The bar is divided into three sections, including a non-smoking eating area. A wide choice of food includes ham and eggs, fillet of pork in a grain mustard sauce, and chicken breast stuffed with spinach and feta cheese. There are also lighter snacks. Regular beers are Theakston's Best Bitter and Morland Old Speckled Hen. Two guest beers are usually available as well.

Distance: *7½ miles*

OS Explorer 222 Rugby & Daventry
GR 581661

A fairly challenging walk, with some long climbs towards the end of the route

Starting point: The car park at the White Horse. Please check with the landlord before leaving your car whilst walking.

How to get there: Welton is situated a mile to the north of Daventry, between the A361 and the A5. The pub is on High Street.

Opening times are 12 noon to 2.30 pm and 7 pm to 11 pm on Monday to Wednesday, 12 noon to 2.30 pm and 6 pm to 11 pm on Thursday and Friday, 12 noon to 3 pm and 6 pm to 11 pm on Saturday, and 12 noon to 3 pm and 7 pm to 10.30 pm on Sunday. Food is served from 12 noon to 2 pm (2.30 pm on Sunday) and 7 pm to 9 pm throughout the week.

Telephone: 01327 702820.

The Walk

1 Leave the front of the pub and turn right. Take the first signed path on your right, then go over a stile and head slightly left, keeping trees to your left. Go over a stile near the bottom of a slope and bear slightly right along the edge of a field. Cross a narrow road and head half-left along a signed path. Cross a stile and footbridge at the far side of a field, then head diagonally right to go through a wooden gate. Walk ahead, keeping a hedge to your right. Follow the path round to the right, then cross a footbridge over a stream and continue. Cross a field to reach a bridge spanning the Grand Union Canal.

2 Turn right immediately after crossing the bridge and walk along the towpath, with the canal to your right. Pass under a road bridge and continue on the towpath, where you may be lucky enough to see a kingfisher. Further on, you reach the impressive Braunston Tunnel. The canal flows through it but there is no towpath, so walk up an incline to the left of the tunnel and continue straight on. Later, the path becomes a well-surfaced track, which curves slightly to the left before bringing you to the A361.

3 Cross the road with care and follow the signed bridleway on the opposite side. Walk up an incline and follow the wide track as it curves slightly to the right. As you begin to drop downhill, there are great views ahead of you towards Braunston. Continue along the path, where ventilation shafts rise out of the ground from the tunnel below. Walk downhill and descend wooden steps on your right, where you reach the far end of Braunston Tunnel.

4 Turn left to rejoin the towpath, with the canal to your right once more. After

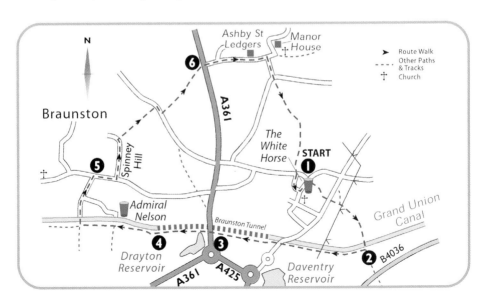

passing locks, walk under a stone bridge and continue ahead. Walk under a bridge by the Admiral Nelson pub and continue on the towpath. Pass a canalside shop by locks and then leave the towpath. Turn right to cross a bridge over the canal, where there are good views to the left and right. Bear round to the right and walk up an incline on a well-surfaced track. At the top of the track, bear slightly left and walk up a narrow lane. Bear right at a fork in the lane to reach a wider road.

❺ Cross the road and turn right, then bear left up Spinney Hill. At the top of the hill, turn right along a wide track, where there are good views to your left. Go through a gate at the end of the track and continue up a gentle incline, with a hedge to your right. Go through another gate and continue. Turn right along a lane, then turn left after about 50 yards and continue on the Jurassic Way. The path drops downhill and you pass trees on your right to arrive at the A361.

❻ Cross the road with caution and walk ahead through the village of Ashby St Ledgers. After passing the village hall, you can see the church and a manor house over to your left. A room at the entrance gate of the house was where Robert Catesby and Guy Fawkes hatched the notorious Gunpowder Plot. Just before reaching the church, turn right along the road. At a fork in the road, go over a stile and head slightly left. Turn diagonally left

The lock on the Grand Union Canal, near point 4

at the far side of a field and walk downhill, then cross a footbridge and bear slightly right to walk up an incline. Continue across a field and go through a gap in the hedge on your left, then turn right. Turn left after a few yards along a clearly-defined path. Drop downhill and then walk uphill, before following the path round to the right. Turn left along a road and turn right along Round Close. Follow the road round to the left, where you will see the White Horse in front of you.

Date walk completed:

....

Place of Interest
Daventry Country Park is a mile south of Welton. The park covers 140 acres and has a reservoir, adventure playground, café, picnic areas, birdwatching hides and guided walks. Open year round. Telephone: 01327 877193.

Great Brington
The Althorp Coaching Inn

This walk starts in the attractive village of Great Brington – an ancient agricultural parish first noted in 1086. Soon after leaving the pub,

you pass close to Althorp House, the ancestral home of the Spencer family, including Diana, Princess of Wales, for nearly 500 years. The route then takes you over rolling countryside, as you pass scenic woodland and streams, before returning to the starting point along quiet tracks and country lanes.

The Althorp Coaching Inn, also known as the Fox and Hounds, dates back to the 16th century. Inside you will find a warm and friendly atmosphere. There is a large bar with flagstone floors and beamed ceilings, as well as a separate eating area and a cellar restaurant. Outside there is a courtyard and an enclosed garden. Food includes snacks like jacket potatoes and baguettes, through to main meals such as venison in a red wine sauce, and baked salmon wrapped in smoked bacon. Regular ales are Greene King IPA and Abbot Ale, Morland Old Speckled Hen and Fuller's London Pride. At least four guest beers are also available.

Opening times are 11 am to 11 pm on Monday to Saturday, and 12 noon to 10.30 pm on Sunday. Food is served from 12 noon to 2.30 pm and 6.30 pm to 9.30 pm on Monday to Friday, 12 noon to 2.30 pm and 6.30 pm to 10 pm on Saturday, and 12 noon to 3 pm and 6.30 pm to 8.30 pm on Sunday.

Telephone: 01604 770651.

Distance: *4 miles*

OS Explorer 223 Northampton & Market Harborough
GR 666649

An easy walk over gently rolling ground

Starting point: The Althorp Coaching Inn's car park (off Back Lane, at the rear of the building). Please ask the landlord for permission to leave your car whilst walking.

How to get there: Great Brington lies to the east of the A5 and the M1 near Daventry. From Northampton, head north-west on the A428. Pass the Althorp Estate on your left, then turn left along an unclassified road to Great Brington. The pub can be found on Main Street.

The Walk

1 Leave the front entrance of the pub and turn right. Where the road bends to the right, turn left along Hamilton Lane. Continue and go through a gate, before walking straight ahead across a grassy field. Go over a stile and bear slightly right. Cross a track further on, where the Althorp Estate can be seen to your left. Continue on a well-defined track, which takes you up a gentle incline. Cross a stile and look back for some good views. Walk straight ahead, passing a wood to your left, then cross a stile to arrive at a road.

2 Turn right along the road and continue to a T-junction. Turn left and walk along the road, paying attention to any oncoming traffic. After 220 yards, turn right along a signed bridleway, which, at this point, is a narrow lane. At the end of the lane go through a gate and bear slightly left. Continue ahead and keep a hedge to your right further on. Go through a gate and bear slightly right, then pass between two gateposts and turn right, to follow an arrow marked 'Midshires Way'. Go through another gate further on and keep straight ahead across a grassy field. To your left and right is a decommissioned firing range, where targets can be seen to your left. Cross a footbridge by a gap in the hedge in front of you, then bear slightly left, to aim for an iron gate.

3 On reaching the gate, turn right and walk along the edge of a field, keeping a hedge to your left. At the end of the field, go through an iron gate on your left and then turn immediately right. Continue, with a drainage ditch and a hedge to your right. Further on, the muddy track

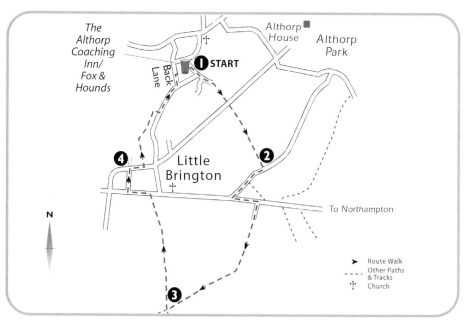

15

Looking back towards the Althorp Estate, near Great Brington

becomes a well-surfaced byway. Continue ahead and walk up an incline to reach a road, from where there are sweeping views behind you. Turn left along the road and then turn right along the next road. Walk downhill to a crossroads.

4 Turn right here and walk along Main Street, passing through the pretty village of Little Brington. Pass Ye Olde Saracen's Head and, soon after, go through a kissing gate on your left, to follow a signed path. Cross a footbridge and bear slightly left. At the top of a slope, go through a kissing gate and bear half-right along a signed bridleway. Drop downhill and cross a footbridge, then turn diagonally right. As you reach a hedge, turn left and walk up a gentle incline, with the hedge to your right. Follow the path, which runs parallel with the road to your right, then go through a kissing gate on your right. Cross the road and turn left along the pavement. Follow the road as it bends to

the right, then turn left along Back Lane. After 70 yards, turn right to return to the pub car park. Alternatively, walk past Back Lane and then follow the main road round to the left, to return to the front entrance of the pub.

Place of Interest
Althorp House is situated a mile to the east of the village. The magnificent grounds are the final resting place of Diana, Princess of Wales. Visitors can enjoy fine architecture, art and sculpture. There is also a wonderful exhibition celebrating the life and work of the Princess. Open between 1st July and 30th September (closed on 31st August). Telephone: 01604 770107.

Date walk completed:

....

16

Eastcote 4 Walk
The Eastcote Arms

The quiet rural village of Eastcote enjoys life at a relaxed pace and is set amid beautiful rolling countryside. After walking through meadows and over brooks, this enjoyable route takes you beside the Grand Union Canal, which is particularly attractive during spring and summer. Later, there is a short climb up to higher ground, where you can take in far-reaching views across the landscape, before making your way back to the start through yet more scenic surroundings.

The Eastcote Arms is a lovely old stone building, with two bars and a non-smoking dining room. There is a friendly and relaxed atmosphere. A wide choice of food is served, and some examples are home-made lasagne and lamb cutlets with a honey and mustard glaze, also snacks such as sandwiches and jacket potatoes. Regular beers are Adnams Bitter, Greene King IPA, Hook Norton Best Bitter and Timothy Taylor Landlord, alongside a regularly changing guest ale. A beer garden at the rear can be enjoyed in fine weather.

Opening times are 12 noon to 3 pm and 6 pm to 11 pm on Monday to Thursday, 12 noon to 11 pm on Friday and Saturday, and 12 noon to 10.30 pm on Sunday. Food is available from 12 noon to 2.30 pm and 6.30 pm to 9.30 pm on Tuesday to Saturday, and 12 noon to 3 pm and 7 pm to 9.30 pm on Sunday (no food on Monday).

Telephone: 01327 830731.

Distance: *5½ miles*

OS Explorer 207 Newport Pagnell & Northampton South
GR 680540

A moderate walk over gently undulating terrain

Starting point: The car park at the Eastcote Arms. Please seek permission from the landlord to leave your car whilst walking.

How to get there: Eastcote lies 4½ miles south-west of Northampton, between the A5 and the A43. The pub can be found on Gayton Road.

The Walk

1 Leave the pub and turn left along the road. Go straight ahead at a crossroads and continue down an incline to a T-junction. Take the signed footpath ahead of you and bear slightly left across a grassy field. Go over a stile and continue, before crossing a footbridge on your left. Once across the bridge, head diagonally right. Go through a gate and bear slightly right, passing under power lines. Cross a footbridge and a stile in quick succession and continue. Where the hedge to your right ends, bear very slightly right and walk up a hill. Cross a stile at the top of the hill and walk straight ahead. Immediately after passing trees to the right, go over a stile on your right and walk ahead. Cross two more stiles and bear slightly left. Pass a house on your left, then go over a stile and head diagonally left, to arrive at a bridge over the railway.

2 Cross the railway bridge and then a bridge over the Grand Union Canal. Immediately after, go over a stile on your left and then go through a gate on your left. Turn left along the canal towpath and pass underneath the bridge, keeping the canal to your right. Continue along the towpath and pass under two road bridges. The canal bends to the right, before you pass under a footbridge. Continue ahead and then turn left by the next bridge (no 43) to reach a road.

3 Turn right and cross the canal bridge. Soon after, go over a level crossing and then turn left along a footpath. This curves slightly to the left, before taking you up an incline. Near the top of the slope, turn right to go through a gap in the hedge and continue ahead. At the far side of a field, bear slightly right and continue, with a hedge to your left. Follow the wide grassy path as it sweeps

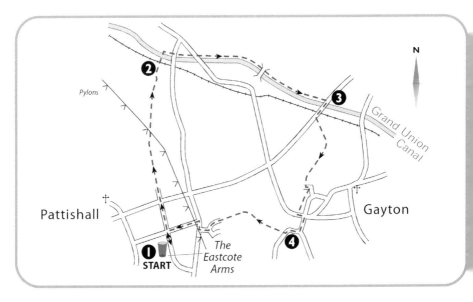

Beautiful rolling countryside near the start of the walk

round to the left. Continue, now with a hedge on either side of the path. At a sharp left-hand bend in the path, turn right along a grassy field and walk ahead until you reach a road. Turn left along the pavement and then turn right at a crossroads. At another road junction, bear round to the right. The road then curves left, bringing you to a signed bridleway.

④ Turn right along the bridleway, which takes you across a field before curving to the right slightly. Drop downhill and cross a footbridge over a brook, then go straight ahead across a field. Further on, follow the path as it bends to the left, taking you between the lines of two hedges. After passing a building on your left, keep straight ahead along a well-surfaced track. At the end of the track, turn right along a road and then turn right

at a T-junction. Immediately after passing Ivy House, turn left along a road. Pass under power lines and then turn left at a crossroads, to return to the pub.

Place of Interest

Situated in converted Victorian buildings, the **Old Dairy Farm Craft Centre** at Upper Stowe is located 3 miles north-west of Eastcote. Lambing weekends and other special events are held, and there are several shops selling unusual items. Work produced by local artists is also on display. Telephone: 01327 340525.

Date walk completed:

....

Stoke Bruerne
The Boat Inn

After walking along country lanes, you then pass through a village with royal connections, before crossing green meadows and a river, to wind your way back to the starting point.

The Boat Inn has been owned by the same family for well over a century and a quarter. It is set in a picturesque canalside location, and regular trips are arranged on the pub's own narrowboat. Inside, the accommodation consists of a lounge bar and two traditional bars, with beamed ceilings and stone floors, also an adjacent bistro and a non-smoking restaurant upstairs. A wide variety of food includes snacks like soup, through to main meals such as fillet steak with Stilton and bacon, and whole lobster thermidor. Regular ales are Marston's Burton Bitter, Pedigree and Old Empire, and Frog Island Best Bitter. At least one guest beer is always available.

This scenic route is particularly enjoyable during the spring and summer months. As soon as you open the back door of the pub you are greeted by the sight of colourful narrowboats. The walk takes you along an attractive stretch of the Grand Union Canal, where you may be lucky enough to see a kingfisher flying low over the water.

Opening times are 9.30 am to 11 pm on Monday to Saturday, and 9.30 am to 10.30 pm on Sunday (closed between 3 pm and 6 pm on Monday to Thursday during winter). Food is served throughout opening hours up to 9.30 pm on Monday to Saturday, and from 9.30 am to 9 pm on Sunday (during winter, last food orders are at 9 pm on Monday to Saturday and 8.30 pm on Sunday).

Telephone: 01604 862428.

Distance: 6¼ miles

OS Explorer 207 Newport Pagnell & Northampton South
GR 743499

An easy walk on mainly flat ground

Starting point: The Boat Inn's car park. Please seek the landlord's permission to leave your car whilst walking.

How to get there: Turn westwards off the A508 along an unclassified road to the south of Northampton and 3 miles from junction 15 of the M1 motorway. The pub can be found on your right, immediately after crossing the bridge over the canal.

The Walk

1 Leave the back door of the pub and turn right by the canal. Cross the road and walk ahead along the towpath, still with the canal to your left. Pass the Navigation pub on the opposite bank and continue past locks. Further on, pass under a bridge carrying the A508 overhead. Turn left and cross a footbridge over the canal, then turn right along the towpath, now with the canal to your right. Further on, a backwater running parallel with the canal can be seen to your left. Pass under a stone bridge

at a bend in the canal and then keep going until you reach the next bridge (no 57).

2 Turn left and walk up some steps beside the bridge, then turn right along the road and cross the bridge. Walk uphill on the road and, as the ground levels, bear round to the left then the right, passing the church on your right-hand side. At a road junction further ahead, turn right along The Lane. You are now in the village of Grafton Regis – famous for being the place where King Edward IV married Elizabeth Woodville in 1464.

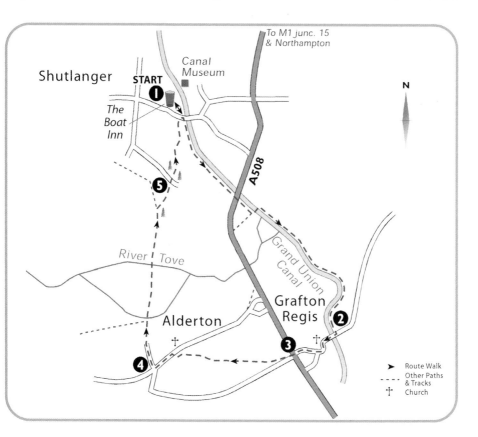

Pass farm buildings on the left and keep straight ahead until you reach the A508.

3 Cross the road with care and go over a stile to follow a signed path, which runs parallel with a narrow lane. After about 100 yards veer to the right slightly, then go over a stile and continue ahead, keeping a hedge to your left. Further on, the path curves to the right then the left. Continue and then turn right at a marker arrow to cross a field. Bear slightly left at the next marker arrow and follow a well-trodden path. Cross a stile and bear slightly left, then cross another stile and bear slightly right. Just before reaching some houses, cross a stile and turn left to arrive at a road. Turn left along the road and walk downhill.

4 Turn right along Spring Lane, passing pretty thatched cottages on the left. Keep going downhill and, where the road runs out, continue straight ahead on a signed bridleway. Cross a field and walk straight on until you reach a gravel track running from left to right. Bear right along the track, then go straight ahead to cross a footbridge over a stream. Head diagonally right and follow the well-trodden bridleway across a grassy field. The path then curves to the left. Cross a bridge over the River Tove and then bear slightly right. Go through a gate at the far side of a field. After a few yards, go over a stile on your right and walk up a gentle incline. After crossing two footbridges spanning streams, bear diagonally left and walk up a gentle slope. Go over a stile and walk straight ahead until you reach a narrow lane.

5 Cross the lane and go through an iron gate, before turning diagonally left along

The Grand Union Canal near Stoke Bruerne

a footpath. As you reach the corner of a barn, bear slightly left and walk between two lines of poplar trees. Go through an iron kissing gate and walk on, keeping a hedge to your left. Pass Stoke Bruerne Nature Reserve on your right, then follow the path round to the left. At this point, the canal is about 30 yards over to your right. Go through a kissing gate and bear round to the right, to arrive at the road, with the bridge to your right. Cross the road and walk straight ahead to arrive back at the pub.

Place of Interest

Stoke Bruerne Canal Museum is situated opposite the pub, beside the canal. Housed in a restored cornmill, it portrays the heritage of inland waterways. There are working models, videos, photographs, colourful designs and a gift shop. Telephone: 01604 862229.

Date walk completed:

....

Sibbertoft

The Red Lion

tracks and paths take you through rural farmland. Later you pass between two reservoirs, where there are wonderful views across the water. After a short stretch along roads, you are accompanied by a delightful babbling brook, before you return through beautiful woodland and fields.

This is a scenic walk that can be enjoyed at any time of year. After leaving the starting point in the attractive village of Sibbertoft, winding

Distance: *5½ miles*

OS Explorer 223 Northampton & Market Harborough
GR 678827

An easy walk on mainly flat ground

Starting point: The Red Lion's car park. Please check with the landlord before leaving your car whilst you walk.

How to get there: Take the A4304 between Market Harborough and Lutterworth. Turn off to the south 4¼ miles from Market Harborough, along an unclassified road into Sibbertoft. Turn right after the church and the pub is on your left, near the end of Welland Rise.

The Red Lion is a cosy village pub with a single bar and a separate non-smoking restaurant. There is also an attractive patio garden for use in fine weather. Food is served throughout, and examples from the menu include steak in Stilton sauce, duck breast on spring onion mash with a red wine jus, and more traditional dishes such as steak and kidney pie. Regular ales come from Adnams and Shepherd Neame.

Opening times are 6.30 pm to 11 pm on Monday and Tuesday, and 12 noon to 3 pm and 6.30 pm to 11 pm on Wednesday to Sunday (10.30 pm on Sunday evening). Food is served from 6.30 pm to 9.30 pm on Monday and Tuesday, and from 12 noon to 2 pm and 6.30 pm to 9.30 pm Wednesday to Sunday.

Telephone: 01858 880011.

The Walk

1 Leave the pub and turn left along the road. At a T-junction, turn right and then follow the road round to the left, passing a white house on your left. Take the path on your left, which is marked 'Jurassic Way', and head diagonally left across a field. Go over a stile and walk diagonally right. At the far side of the field follow a marker post, which directs you to the right. Go through an iron gate and then head half-left, to follow an arrow marked 'Reservoir Walk'. Go over a stile and then walk straight on across a field, until you reach a track.

2 Bear half-right and go through an iron gate, to walk along a well-surfaced track. Keep a hedge to your left and, where the track bends to the left, walk straight on. Go through a kissing gate, then pass a track to your right and continue. At a junction of tracks further on, go straight ahead and then cross a stile on your left.

Turn left and pass close to a farm building on your left-hand side. Walk across a field, then go over a narrow lane and through a kissing gate, before continuing straight ahead. At the far side of a field, climb over some wooden steps and then bear slightly right, aiming for a marker post. Cross a footbridge and a stile, then go straight ahead over a field. The path drops downhill, bringing you to a stile.

3 Cross the stile and walk across a concrete dam, where there are good views of Sulby Reservoir to your left and Welford Reservoir to your right. At the end of the dam, bear right and go through a kissing gate, then turn right and walk along a path. At the end of the reservoir, walk on until you reach a narrow road. Turn right along the road and continue to a T-junction. Turn left and, after about 75 yards, you arrive at a footpath sign marked 'Abbey Walk'.

4 To access this path, turn left and walk

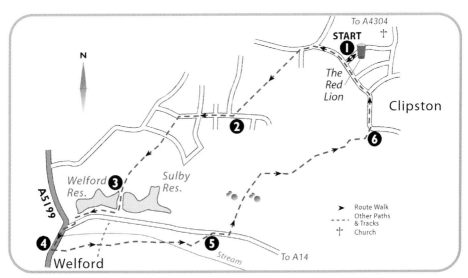

24

along the drive of a house (number 51). Keep left and continue to a stile. Go over the stile and bear slightly right across a field. Soon after, go over a stile and a footbridge, and walk across a field. At a marked junction of paths further on, keep straight ahead. After going through

Looking across the Welford Reservoir

the second of two iron gates, bear slightly left and follow signs marked 'Abbey Walk'. Cross a footbridge over a stream and continue ahead. Go over two stiles in quick succession and continue ahead, keeping a stream to your left. Further on, cross the stream and go through a wooden gate and follow a marked bridleway. Cross a gravel track and then bear slightly left, to walk up a gentle incline. At the far side of a field you arrive at a lane.

5 Turn right along the lane and, after a few yards, turn left along a signed bridleway. Further on, a marker post guides you straight ahead through a stretch of woodland. At the far side of the wood, cross a field and then bear right, passing another wood on your left-hand side. After 200 yards, bear diagonally left along a clearly defined track. Walk up a gentle incline and, at the far side of a field,

a marker post guides you straight ahead. Walk down a gentle incline and then cross a footbridge, before bearing slightly right across a field. At the far side of the field go straight ahead, keeping a drainage ditch to your right. Turn left along a gravel track, which immediately curves to the right. Pass a house on your left, then turn left along the track and continue to a road.

6 Turn left along the road. At a fork in the road further on, take the left-hand branch. Pass houses on your right, then take the second road on your right (Welland Rise) and continue to the starting point at the Red Lion pub.

Date walk completed:

....

Place of Interest
Cottesbrooke Hall and Gardens are situated 5½ miles south of Sibbertoft, just off the A5199. The hall is set in stunning parkland and is a fine example of Queen Anne architecture. It also houses a superb collection of sporting paintings. Telephone: 01604 505808.

Sutton Bassett
The Queen's Head

however, a short climb soon after the start takes you up on to high ground, and from here there are some wonderful views across the countryside. You then walk through grassy meadows before looping back to the starting point.

The **Queen's Head** dates back to around 1893. It has

The tiny village of Sutton Bassett marks the starting point for this short, but enjoyable walk. The route is particularly rewarding during spring and early summer, when the hedgerows are resonant with the sound of birdsong. Much of the terrain is flat;

an upstairs restaurant and two bars, which have beamed ceilings and a real fire in winter. Outside, a patio terrace overlooks the fields. Food is served throughout, and there are snacks such as home-made soup and jacket potatoes, through to main meals like fillet steak in brandy and cream sauce and haddock in beer batter. There are also vegetarian options and a weekly changing specials board. Beers include Timothy Taylor Landlord, Adnams Bitter and Greene King IPA, alongside a varying guest ale.

Distance: *3¼ miles*

OS Explorer 223 Northampton & Market Harborough
GR 770902

An easy walk, with one short, steep climb

Starting point: The car park at the Queen's Head. Please obtain the landlord's permission to leave your car whilst walking.

How to get there: Sutton Bassett is situated 3 miles to the north-east of Market Harborough. The pub can be found on the B664.

Opening times are 12 noon to 2.30 pm and 5 pm to 11 pm on Monday to Friday, 12 noon to 11 pm on Saturday, and 12 noon to 10.30 pm on Sunday. Food is available from 12 noon to 2.30 pm and 6 pm to 9.30 pm on Monday to Friday, and from 12 noon to 9.30 pm on Saturday and Sunday.

Telephone: 01858 463530.

The Walk

1 With the pub behind you, cross over to the opposite side of the road and turn right along the pavement. After 200 yards, turn left and walk between two houses. Go over a stile and follow a signed path, heading slightly left across a field. Cross a stile in a hedgerow and continue straight ahead. At the far side of a field, go over a stile and then walk straight ahead. Keep going up a slope, which gets steeper as you walk. Near the top of the hill, pass underneath a line of electricity pylons and then pass a pond on your left-hand side, before turning right to go through a gate. Continue, passing a cattle-shed on your right. Keep straight ahead, with a hedge to your right. Go through an iron gate at the far side of the field and continue straight ahead. Keep going until you reach a junction of marked paths.

2 Turn right here and go through a gate. From the high ground there are good views ahead of you. Drop downhill, keeping the line of a hedge to your left. At the bottom of the hill, go through a gate and bear round to the right. Keep going as you pass farm buildings and houses on your right-hand side. Follow the metalled track, which eventually curves to the left before bringing you to a road junction.

3 Ignore a lane immediately off to the left, but cross to the opposite side of the main road and then turn left. Walk along the road with care, as it bends round to the right. Take the next signed path on your right-hand side and cross a grassy field. Further on, go through an iron gate and then continue straight ahead, keeping the line of a hedge to your right. Keep going and pass underneath a line of electricity pylons. Shortly before reaching a footbridge over the River Welland, you come to a wooden gate on your right-hand side.

4 Go through the gate and then walk straight ahead across a grassy field. Pass under the line of electricity pylons again and keep straight ahead, aiming for a wide iron gate ahead of you. Go through

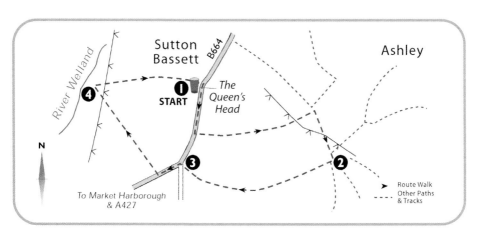

One of the many wonderful views on this walk

the gate and then continue straight ahead, keeping the line of a hedge to your left-hand side. Just before passing a large tree in the hedgerow, veer off to the right and walk up an incline. As the ground levels, go through two gates in quick succession to reach a road. Immediately to your right is the Queen's Head.

Date walk completed:

....

Place of Interest
Rushton Triangular Lodge (English Heritage) is situated 6¼ miles south-east of Sutton Bassett. This small triangular building was designed and built by the Roman Catholic Sir Thomas Tresham, between 1593 and 1597. There are three floors, trefoil windows and three triangular gables on each side. Telephone: 01536 710761.

The Royal Oak

This delightful walk starts and finishes in the historic village of Walgrave. It has some beautiful old houses and an impressive church, and its rural setting makes it an ideal place to enjoy a peaceful day in the countryside. The route takes you through a gently rolling landscape, dotted with woods, farms and streams, and there are plenty of fine views to enjoy along the way.

The Royal Oak is an attractive stone pub with two bars, a separate non-smoking restaurant and a beer garden. There is also an adjacent building where Northamptonshire skittles is played. Food is served throughout, and examples include jacket potatoes, home-made lasagne and fillet of pork. Adnams Bitter is available, alongside four changing guest ales.

Distance: *7¼ miles*

OS Explorer 223 Northampton & Market Harborough
GR 803721

A moderate walk on undulating ground

Starting point: The Royal Oak's car park, but please obtain the landlord's permission to leave your car whilst walking.

How to get there: From the A43 between Kettering and Northampton, turn off south-west 3½ miles from Kettering along an unclassified road to Walgrave, where the pub can be found on your right.

Opening times are 12 noon to 3 pm and 5.30 pm to 11 pm on Monday to Thursday, 12 noon to 3 pm and 5 pm to 11 pm on Friday and Saturday, and 12 noon to 10.30 pm on Sunday. Food is served from 12 noon to 2 pm and 6.30 pm to 9 pm on Monday to Thursday, 12 noon to 2 pm and 6.30 pm to 9.30 pm on Friday and Saturday, and 12 noon to 5 pm on Sunday.

Telephone: 01604 781248.

The Walk

1 Turn right out of the pub and then turn left along a road past the village green. Bear left again and continue along the road, passing over a stream further ahead. Walk up a gentle incline and pass Hall Farm, then turn left along the next signed path, keeping trees to your left. At the end of a field, go over a stile and bear slightly left. Cross a footbridge and then bear to the right and go over another stile. Bear slightly left here and cross a field. Go over a stile and head diagonally left to cross a footbridge over a stream, then head diagonally right and walk up an incline to a road.

2 Turn right along the road and, after about 75 yards, go through an iron gate on your left to follow a signed path. Continue ahead, with a dyke to your left.

Further on, a marker arrow near a footbridge guides you straight on. Pass another bridge and walk ahead, keeping a hedge to your left. Turn left to cross a stone footbridge, then turn immediately right. After a few yards, a marker post guides you slightly left across a field. Cross a footbridge over a ditch and walk across a field, then cross a metalled track, before continuing ahead. At the far side of a field, go over a footbridge to arrive at an unmarked bridleway.

3 Turn left here and continue between attractive hedgerows and trees. Follow the track as it curves gently to the left. Further on, pass between two concrete posts on either side of the track and then bear round to the right to reach a road. Turn left and walk along the road, paying attention to any oncoming traffic. Continue as the road bends to the right.

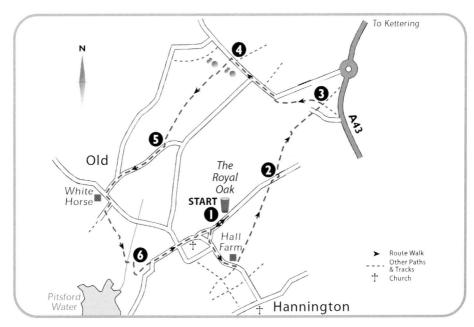

Ignore a road off to the left further on, but keep straight ahead and pass houses on your right.

4 Turn left along the next signed path and pass a radio mast on your right. Walk through a stretch of woodland, ignoring unmarked paths off to the left and right. At the far edge of the wood, turn right then immediately left, to follow a marked path straight ahead. At the far side of a field, cross a footbridge over a ditch and head diagonally right. A marker post in the corner of a field then guides you straight ahead. Keep a hedge to your right and enjoy fine views across the countryside to your left. Pass several small ponds to your left and continue ahead until you reach a road.

5 Turn right along the road and walk downhill. Pass through the pretty village of Old and continue to a T-junction, with the White Horse pub ahead of you. Turn left here, and walk up a gentle incline. Turn right along Bridle Road and then go over a stile on your left. Follow the signed path heading diagonally right across a grassy field, then go over a stile and continue in the same direction. After another stile, turn right along a track, continuing for 50 yards to reach an iron gate and head diagonally left. Cross a grassy field and then go over a stile to arrive at a junction of tracks. Turn left, keeping a hedge to your left-hand side. At the end of a field, turn right to follow a marker post, keeping a hedge to your right. The path takes you down an incline, before curving to the left.

6 At the bottom of the slope, turn right along an unmarked path, keeping a stream to your left. After about 300

Looking back along the track on the homeward stretch

yards, turn left and cross a footbridge over the stream. Walk up an incline, with a hedge to your right. As the ground levels, look back for some fine views. On reaching a road further on, walk straight ahead along the pavement. Continue past attractive houses and the church on your right. Pass the tiny village green on your right and then walk on, to retrace your steps back to the pub.

Place of Interest

Cottesbrooke Hall and Gardens are located 5½ miles west of Walgrave. The hall is set in beautiful parkland and is an excellent example of Queen Anne architecture. It is also home to a superb collection of sporting paintings. Telephone: 01604 505808.

Date walk completed:

....

Grendon
The Half Moon

houses and cottages – some with thatched roofs – provide a picturesque backdrop to the start of this enjoyable route. You pass through open fields and trace the line of a clear brook for some distance, before crossing bridges over streams. After a gradual climb, you wind your way back to the village along narrow lanes.

Grendon is not unlike some of the villages to be found in the Cotswolds. Its attractive stone

Distance: *3¾ miles*

OS Explorer 207 Newport Pagnell & Northampton South
GR 880606

An easy walk, with a few gradual slopes

Starting point: The car park at the Half Moon. Please check with the landlord before leaving your car whilst walking.

How to get there: Grendon is located 4½ miles south of Wellingborough, between the A45 and the A509. From Wellingborough, head south on the A5193 and continue south on the A509. At a traffic island on the outskirts of Wollaston, turn right along an unclassified road, then turn left into Grendon, where the pub can be found on Main Road.

The Half Moon is an attractive building with a thatched roof and a beer garden at the rear. Inside there is a large main bar with a dedicated non-smoking area. Low-beamed ceilings help to enhance the cosy atmosphere. Food includes snacks like sandwiches and baked potatoes, through to main meals such as lemon sole or spinach and mushroom lasagne. Regular ales are Charles Wells Eagle and Bombardier, which are served alongside a changing guest beer.

Opening times are 12 noon to 2.30 pm and 6 pm to 11 pm on Monday to Friday, 12 noon to 3 pm and 6.30 pm to 11 pm on Saturday, and 12 noon to 3 pm and 7 pm to 10.30 pm on Sunday. Food is served from 12 noon to 2 pm and 7 pm to 9.15 pm on Monday to Saturday, and 12 noon to 2 pm on Sunday.

Telephone: 01933 663263.

The Walk

1 Turn right out of the pub and pass the village hall soon after. Cross a stile on your right and follow a signed path straight ahead. Go through an iron gate and continue, keeping a hedge to your right. As you reach an iron gate on your right, turn diagonally left along an unmarked track. Cross a footbridge over a stream and then bear half-right across a field, to pass underneath power lines.

2 At the end of the field, go through an iron gate and bear slightly right, keeping a hedge to your right. At the end of the hedge, head slightly right again across a grassy field. Cross a stile and follow a marker arrow, which guides you diagonally right. Cross a footbridge further on and then bear a little to the right across a grassy field. Cross a footbridge and head slightly right, with a brook to your right. Follow the path as it curves to the right and left, then cross a footbridge at the end of a field. Walk straight ahead and then follow the path round to the left. At a marker post by a junction of tracks, bear round to the right then the left. Pass a footbridge on your right and continue ahead, still with the brook to your right. At the edge of the field, a marker post guides you straight on. Continue, keeping a hedge to your right. Go through a gate and walk on until you reach a footbridge on your right.

3 Cross the bridge and head diagonally right across a grassy field. Go over a stile in the hedgerow and then walk straight ahead. To your left you can see the ancient church at Easton Maudit. At a junction of marked tracks, cross a footbridge and bear slightly right across a field. Cross a track near a derelict building and bear slightly right. Further on, cross another footbridge over a stream and head slightly right, to walk up a gentle incline. Enjoy the views at the top of the slope, then bear slightly left to go through a gap in the hedge. Continue ahead, with a hedge to your right. Go over a stile and walk on,

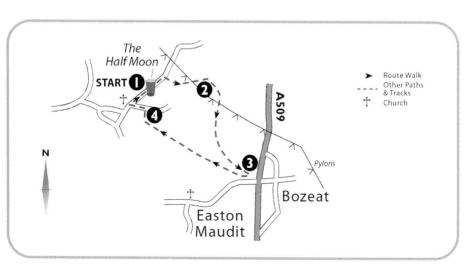

The stream near the beginning of the walk

then go over a stile on your right and walk straight ahead along an unmarked path. Go through a kissing gate to reach a lane.

4 Turn left along the lane and walk up an incline, heading towards the church. Turn right at the top of the lane and pass the impressive St Mary's church on your left-hand side. Walk downhill, with attractive houses on both sides of the road. Soon you return to the Half Moon pub on your right.

Date walk completed:

....

Place of Interest

Castle Ashby Gardens offer a variety of attractive garden styles dating back to 1695. There are also Victorian terrace gardens and an Italian conservatory. The adjacent stately home (built in 1574) is not open to the public, except for weddings and functions. The gardens are open year round and are located a mile to the south-west of Grendon. Telephone: 01604 696696.

The Duke's Arms

walk beside the River Nene. Later, you pass tranquil lakes and cross bridges over the river. Towards the end of the circuit, there are good views from elevated ground over the Nene Valley.

The Duke's Arms dates back to the 17th century. It is named after Duke of Wellington, who used to visit the pub when staying in the village. Previously known as the Lord's Arms, it is said that the 19th-century landlord changed the name in honour of his famous customer. Inside you will find a large bar, two non-smoking restaurants and a separate games room. Snacks such as jacket potatoes and sandwiches are served, as well as main meals like fillet steak and curries. There is also a carvery. Regular beers are Greene King IPA, Fuller's London Pride and Hop Back Summer Lightning, alongside two changing guest ales. There is a beer garden at the rear of the pub.

The village of Woodford has a long history, and there are still a few houses standing which date back to the 1300s. The route takes you to the site of the old medieval village, before you

Distance: 4¼ miles

OS Explorer 224 Corby, Kettering & Wellingborough
GR 967770

An easy walk on mainly flat ground

Starting point: The car park at the Duke's Arms. Please obtain the landlord's permission to leave your car whilst walking.

How to get there: Woodford is 5½ miles east of Kettering, off the A14. The pub is on High Street, overlooking the village green.

Opening times are 7 pm to 11 pm on Monday, 12 noon to 3 pm and 7 pm to 11 pm on Tuesday to Saturday, and 12 noon to 10.30 pm on Sunday. Food is served from 12 noon to 2.30 pm and 7.30 pm to 9 pm (but not on Monday lunchtime or Sunday evening).

Telephone: 01832 732224.

35

The Walk

1 Leave the main entrance of the pub and turn left. Turn right after a few yards and pass the village green on your right. Turn left along a signed path after 200 yards and go through a kissing gate, before turning diagonally right. Go through another kissing gate and continue in the same direction. The medieval village of Woodford once stood in this area. At the bottom of a slope, go over a stile and bear diagonally right along a grassy track, where the River Nene can be seen to your left. Follow the path as it curves to the right, then continue ahead along the Nene Way. Cross a well-surfaced track further on and continue straight ahead. Go through a kissing gate and bear half-right to walk up a slope, then go over a stile and stay on the Nene Way. Cross a dismantled railway and continue ahead, then go over a stile and veer round to the right to arrive at a bend in the road.

2 Turn left along the road and cross two bridges over the River Nene. Continue with care and pass between two attractive lakes. Where the main road bends sharply to the left, turn right along a narrow lane. At the end of the lane, continue round to the right along a track (the Nene Way). Cross a bridge over a narrow stretch of water and then follow the path round to the left. Soon after, the River Nene branches off into three sections. Cross a bridge over the first fork of the river and another soon after, then cross a third bridge slightly to your right and continue. Turn left after 90 yards and, as you reach a footbridge, turn right. Continue with a stream to your left and turn right at the corner of a field. After 200 yards, turn left along a well-trodden path. Take the next marked path on your right and continue with a hedge to your left. Further on, go through a gap in the hedge and continue, now with a hedge to your right. At a junction of tracks, walk ahead to reach a road.

3 Cross the road and continue along the path. Follow it round to the right, then go over a stile on your left. Immediately afterwards, go over a stile on your right.

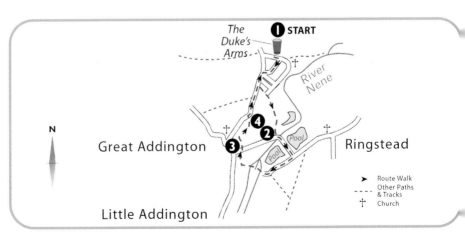

The River Nene near Woodford

and walk up a gentle incline, keeping a hedge to your right. At the top of the slope, go through a gap in the hedge and then bear diagonally left across a field. To your right there are good views towards Woodford. Go over a stile to arrive at a road.

4 Turn right along the road and follow it as it curves to the right. As you drop downhill, there are good views to your right across the Nene Valley. Before approaching a right-hand bend in the road, you may wish to change sides in order to maintain a clear view of oncoming traffic. Further on, pass a path on your right, which was used at the start of the walk. Continue past the village green on your left, before returning to the pub.

Date walk completed:

....

Place of Interest
Boughton House is located 5½ miles to the north-west of Woodford. Visitors can see fine furniture, art, porcelain and ornaments. There are also beautiful grounds to explore, which are managed with conservation in mind. The park is open from May to September and the house is open from August to September. Telephone: 01536 515731.

The King's Head

there are some fantastic views across the Nene Valley. Further on there are country lanes and you walk through a beautiful nature reserve, owned by Northamptonshire Wildlife Trust. You also pass an old mill and a trout fishery, before heading back to the starting point.

The King's Head is a beautiful building dating back to 1662. It is situated close to the River Nene and is popular with walkers and locals alike. There are two bars with inglenook fireplaces and quarry-tiled floors, and two separate non-smoking dining rooms. Food is served throughout and examples from the regularly changing menus might include chilli and rice, chicken breast with a Stilton and brandy jus, or one of the many seafood specials. Regular ales are Adnams Bitter and Timothy Taylor Landlord. Various guest beers are also available, and there is a beer garden at the rear of the building.

Opening times are 12 noon to 2.30 pm and 7 pm to 11 pm on Monday and Tuesday, 12 noon to 2.30 pm and 6.30 pm to 11 pm on Wednesday to Saturday, and 12 noon to 4 pm on Sunday (closed on Tuesday in winter and open all day Saturday and Sunday in summer) Food is available from 12 noon to 2 pm and 7 pm to 9 pm on Monday to Sunday.

Telephone: 01832 720024.

T his walk starts in the idyllic village of Wadenhoe, with its charming thatched cottages and picturesque stone houses. The route takes you beside a peaceful stretch of the River Nene and then onto higher ground, from where

Distance: 6½ miles

OS Explorer 224 Corby, Kettering & Wellingborough
GR 011834

An easy walk on mainly flat ground

Starting point: The car park at the King's Head. Please seek the landlord's permission to leave your car whilst walking.

How to get there: Wadenhoe is 3 miles north of Thrapston, off the A605. The pub is at the end of Church Street, close to the river.

The Walk

1 Leave the pub and turn left along the road. Go through a gate and bear slightly left, to arrive at a marker post. Walk straight ahead along the Nene Way, with the River Nene to your left. Go through a gate and continue, with the church to your right. Further on, bear slightly right and walk up an incline, along a well-defined track. Cross two footbridges in quick succession and follow the Nene Way. Walk through a wooded area and follow the path as it bends slightly to the left. Cross a footbridge and go through a gate immediately after, before continuing on the main path. At the end of the wooded area go over a stile and walk across a field, then cross a footbridge over a stream and walk up an incline. Pass a stile on your left and continue ahead.

Turn half-left at a junction of tracks further on and then go through two kissing gates. Bear half-left and cross a footbridge, then head diagonally right along a signed path. Go through a gate and bear right to emerge at a road.

2 Turn left along the road, then turn right down Lowick Lane. Pass houses on both sides and continue, then turn left by a sign marked 'Titchmarsh Reserve'. Turn right and pass a reserve information board, then turn left along a track. Cross a footbridge over a brook and then go through a gate, before turning right along the Nene Way. Walk along the edge of the reserve and pass birdwatching hides on your left. Further on, there are large flooded gravel pits on either side of you. Pass under some power lines and turn left by a stone bridge, then go through a gate

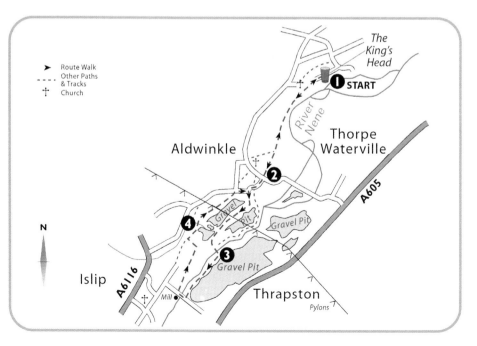

to leave the reserve. Turn left and cross a bridge over the River Nene to arrive at a well-surfaced track.

❸ Turn right along the track and continue past a sailing club on your left. Soon after, turn right and cross a bridge over the river, which takes you past an old mill. Soon after, turn right and follow a path marked 'Nene Way Footpath'. Cross a footbridge spanning a drainage ditch and continue ahead. At the edge of a wood, turn left along a signed footpath, then turn right along a marked public byway and continue to a footbridge.

❹ Cross the bridge and aim diagonally left to follow a signed footpath across a grassy field. Soon after passing under power lines, veer slightly right along a well-trodden path. To your right is an attractive flooded gravel pit, which is used for trout fishing. Further on, go through an iron gate and pass an old farm building on your left. Follow the track round to the left, where there are good views over to your right. Keep going until you reach a narrow road. Turn right along the road, then follow it round to the left. Further on, pass the path marked 'Titchmarsh Reserve', which was encountered earlier on the walk. Walk back along Lowick Lane and turn left at the T-junction. Take the next path on your right and go through a gate, before bearing half-left

Titchmarsh Nature Reserve near Wadenhoe

across a field. Cross the footbridge used earlier and bear half-right to go through the kissing gates. Head diagonally left across the field to the junction of marked tracks encountered earlier. From here, retrace your steps back across fields and through the stretch of woodland, then pass the church on your left and carry on back to the pub.

Date walk completed:

....

Place of Interest

Lyveden New Bield (National Trust) is situated 2 miles north-west of Wadenhoe. This incomplete Elizabethan garden house and moated garden was started in 1595 by Sir Thomas Tresham, and has remained virtually unchanged since work stopped in 1605. It boasts one of the oldest garden layouts in Britain. Telephone: 01832 205358.

The Queen's Head

This rewarding walk starts in the pretty village of Bulwick, with its honey-coloured stone houses and thatched cottages. Along the way, you pass through gently rolling woodland, where there is an opportunity to see rare birds of prey gliding overhead. You also walk through the grounds of a beautiful country estate, before returning along the banks of a tranquil brook.

The Queen's Head is an attractive building, parts of which date back to 1645. There is a main bar and a three-roomed non-smoking restaurant. Food is served throughout the pub, and examples include dishes such as onion and red pepper soup, smoked salmon and ginger fishcakes and rack of English lamb. Shepherd Neame Spitfire is a regular at the pumps, and guest beers are from local brewers like Rockingham Ales and Newby Wyke Brewery.

Opening times are 12 noon to 3 pm and 6 pm to 11 pm on Tuesday to Saturday, and 12 noon to 4 pm and 7 pm to 10.30 pm on Sunday (closed all day Monday). Food is served from 12 noon to 2.30 pm and 6 pm to 9.30 pm on Tuesday to Saturday, and from 12 noon to 3.30 pm on Sunday.

Telephone: 01780 450272.

Distance: *7 miles*

OS Explorer 224 Corby, Kettering & Wellingborough
GR 962942

A moderate walk; muddy in places

Starting point: The car park at the Queen's Head. Please seek the landlord's permission to leave your car whilst walking.

How to get there: Bulwick is 5½ miles north-east of Corby, just off the A43. The pub is opposite the church.

The Walk

1 With the pub behind you, cross the road and walk along a lane, then bear slightly left to pass the churchyard on your left. Go over a stile on your right and then through a gate. Bear slightly left and cross a stile. Pass a house on your right, then go over another stile to arrive at a lane. Cross the lane and follow the signed footpath diagonally left. At the far side of a field, walk up a gentle incline and then cross a stile on your left. Turn immediately right and continue with a hedge to your right. Go through a gap in the hedge and turn immediately left. At a marker post go straight ahead, aiming for the right-hand corner of a wood.

2 On reaching the wood, turn left then immediately right, to cross a narrow drainage ditch. At the corner of a field, go straight ahead on an unmarked path. Cross a footbridge at the far side of the field and head diagonally left. Go over a stile and turn left. After passing a disused farm building to your left, turn right and walk up an incline. Go through a gate and continue straight ahead, keeping a hedge to your right. Where the hedge runs out, bear half-right across a field and aim for the right-hand edge of a wood.

3 At the far side of the field, turn right and right again. Keep a hedge to your right and go through a kissing gate further on. At the top of a slope, go through an iron gate and continue. As you approach a strip of woodland ahead, you are likely to see red kites swirling overhead. These magnificent birds of prey were once extinct in England, but after a reintroduction programme they are now flourishing again. Pass the wood on your

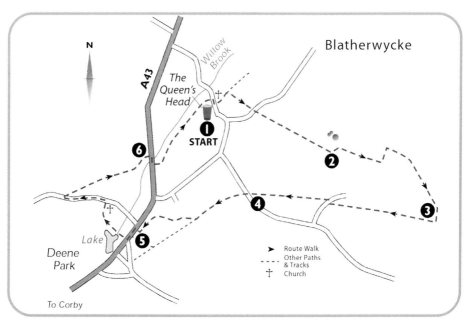

left and walk through a farmyard. At the end of the yard, turn right then immediately left along a well-surfaced track. Continue straight ahead on the bridleway to a narrow lane.

4 Cross the lane to follow a signed bridleway across a field. Walk down a slope and cross a footbridge. Soon after, veer off to the right on an unmarked path. Pass a small wood immediately to your right and cross a wooden footbridge on your left. Turn immediately right and follow the path round to the right, then cross a footbridge and walk over a field. Go through a gap in the hedge and continue straight ahead over another field. Veer slightly right and aim for a marker post, then walk down a gentle slope. Continue straight ahead, keeping a hedge to your right. At the end of a field bear left, keeping a wooden fence to your right. Soon you reach a main road.

5 Cross the road and turn left. Walk along the road with care and take the signed path on your right. Walk along a line of trees in the grounds of Deene Park. Cross a footbridge and pass a lake on your left. Soon after, follow the path round to the left. Continue to the right and follow the path through a churchyard to the road. Turn left along the road and, after 220 yards, take the signed public footpath on the right. Pass a needle-shaped monument on the left, then go over a stile and walk straight ahead. Cross another stile and go straight ahead. Pass a brick hut on your right and go through a marshy area to cross a stile. Continue ahead and cross a footbridge, then pass through a wooded area. Follow the path round to the right, then cross a footbridge and a stile to reach a main road.

Keep a look-out for red kites swirling overhead

6 Turn right and walk along the road with care. After about 40 yards, cross the road and follow a signed path. Cross a stile and then turn left at the edge of a field, keeping a stream to your left. Further on, go over a stile and continue. On reaching a small wood ahead of you, ignore a stile on your left, but walk straight ahead. Further on, go over a stile beside a gate and continue, to find yourself back at the Queen's Head.

Places of Interest
Deene Park, which is passed on the route, is a 16th-century house incorporating a medieval manor. It was the seat of the Earls of Cardigan, and houses paintings, possessions and memorabilia of the Crimean War. Telephone: 01780 450278.
Kirby Hall is situated 2½ miles south-west of the village. The richly-carved Elizabethan house and ornate gardens are managed by English Heritage. Telephone: 01536 203230.

Date walk completed:

43

The Millstone Inn

This circuit starts in the picturesque village of Barnack, tucked away in the north-west corner of Cambridgeshire. The route takes you along well-marked paths and tracks, and affords some fine views of the surrounding countryside. After strolling through meadows and along country lanes, you follow the course of a Roman road. Soon after, the walk leads you through a National Nature Reserve, which is home to a variety of rare flowers, insects and other animals.

The Millstone Inn is an attractive pub with a friendly atmosphere. Built from local limestone, parts of it date back to 1672. Inside you will find a main bar and three separate non-smoking eating areas. A wide choice of food is available, from sandwiches to main meals like home-made fish pie, broccoli and cream cheese bake and fillet steak. Regular ales are Everards Tiger and Original, and Adnams Bitter. There is also a regularly changing guest beer. A walled beer garden can be enjoyed in fine weather.

Opening times are 11.30 am to 2.30 pm and 5 pm to 11 pm on Monday to Thursday, 11.30 am to 3 pm and 5 pm to 11 pm on Friday, 11.30 am to 11 pm on Saturday, and 12 noon to 10.30 pm on Sunday. Food is available from 11.30 am to 2.15 pm and 6 pm to 9 pm on Monday to Thursday, 11.30 am to 2.30 pm and 5.30 pm to 9.30 pm on Friday and Saturday, and 12 noon to 8.30 pm on Sunday.

Telephone: 01780 740296.

Distance: *3¾ miles*

OS Explorer 234 Rutland Water
GR 076049

An easy walk on largely flat ground

Starting point: The Millstone Inn's car park. Please obtain the landlord's permission to leave your car whilst walking.

How to get there: Barnack is located off the B1443, west of Peterborough. The pub can be found on Millstone Lane, off Main Street.

The Walk

1 Leave the pub car park and turn left. At the end of Millstone Lane turn right and then turn right again at a T-junction. Follow the road round to the left and take a signed path on your right, opposite the church. The well-surfaced path becomes a muddy track as you continue. As you reach two wooden posts on either side of the track, bear half-right along a signed path, keeping a stone wall to your right. Pass a field on your left and go through a kissing gate ahead of you. Walk straight on and, where the fence to your left ends, bear slightly left. Go through a kissing gate and turn left along a road. Turn right after 40 yards to follow a signed path across a field, then go over a stile and continue ahead. Go over another stile by a house to reach a road.

2 Walk straight ahead along the road, passing houses on either side of you. On your right-hand side further ahead, you pass several blocks of Barnack limestone lying on an area of grass beside the pavement. They fell from carts during transport to the River Nene sometime before 1450, and were intended to be used in the construction of Peterborough and Ely cathedrals. Walk ahead and turn

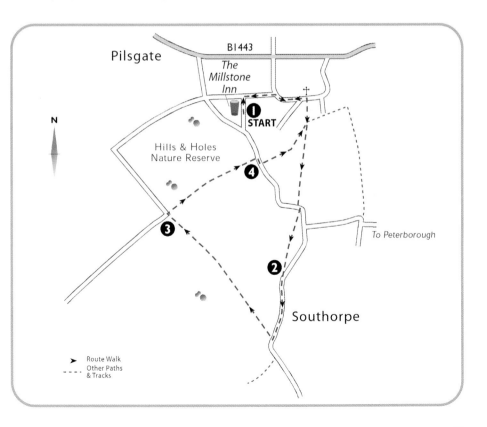

right along a signed bridleway, which follows the course of a Roman road known as Ermine Street. Continue up a gentle incline and go through a kissing gate at the far side of a grassy field, then walk straight ahead. Further on, keep straight ahead along a gravel track. Continue with the line of a stone wall to your right. Further on, a gap in the wall allows a glimpse of Walcot Hall and its impressive grounds. Go through a kissing gate to arrive at a road.

The Hills and Holes Nature Reserve is passed on the walk

❸ Turn immediately right and walk along a signed path, keeping a stone wall to your right. Go through a kissing gate further on to enter the Hills and Holes National Nature Reserve. The hills and holes, which can be seen on the ground to the left of the path, are the remains of limestone workings first used by the Romans. Continue straight ahead along the path. Further on, you may wish to explore the reserve grassland to your left. In spring and summer, nine different types of wild orchid can be found here and during the evenings the eerie lights of glow-worms can be seen. Continue on the path and go through a kissing gate to reach a road.

❹ Turn right along the road and, after 30 yards, go through a gap in a wall on your left. Walk past a bowling green on your right and then go through another gap in a wall, before turning left. Pass along the line of a stone wall to your left, on a path used near the start of the walk. Further on, bear left along the path used earlier and continue to the road. Turn left and pass the church on your right-hand side. Follow the road round to the right, then turn left along Main Street and left along Millstone Lane, where you return to the starting point.

Place of Interest

Burghley Park is situated 2 miles north-west of Barnack. The beautiful grounds were laid out by Capability Brown, and at the heart of the estate is a fine Elizabethan mansion, which was built between 1555 and 1587. Telephone: 01780 752451.

Date walk completed:

....

46

The Bell Inn

Stilton stands close to the course of a Roman road, and this exhilarating walk is packed with intrigue and history from start to finish. The coaching era, from the 1630s to the 1840s, signalled a period of prosperity for the village, and as the coaches brought more people – and, significantly, mail – Stilton became a major posting stage, supporting around 14 public houses and inns. More history is revealed along the course of the route, as you pass the sites of an ancient fort and an Anglo-Saxon village.

The Bell Inn is a superb building, parts of which date back to the 1500s. Cooper Thornhill was landlord at the inn from 1730 to 1759 and is credited with popularising the famous Stilton cheese, which he served there. Despite its name, most agree that it was never actually made in the village (see Walk 16). Meals are available in the Village Bar, the Bistro

and the award-winning restaurant. There is also a courtyard and beer garden at the rear. Dishes include such delights as Stilton soup, and fillet of lemon sole with an aniseed butter sauce. Regular ales come from Fuller's, Oakham and Greene King.

Opening times are 12 noon to 2.30 pm and 6 pm to 11 pm on Monday to Friday, 12 noon to 3 pm and 6 pm to 11 pm on Saturday, and 12 noon to 3 pm and 7 pm to 10.30 pm on Sunday. Food is available from 12 noon to 2 pm and 6.30 pm to 9.30 pm on Monday to Saturday, and from 12 noon to 2 pm and 7 pm to 9 pm on Sunday. The restaurant is closed at lunchtime on Saturday and on Sunday evenings.

Telephone: 01733 241066.

Distance: *7 miles*

OS Explorer 227 Peterborough
GR 163893

A moderate walk, with some gradual slopes; can be muddy in places

Starting point: The Bell Inn's car park (please seek the landlord's permission to leave your car whilst walking), or the road in front of the inn.

How to get there: Stilton is situated 3 miles south of Peterborough, just off the A1(M). The Bell Inn can be found on Great North Road.

The Walk

1 With the pub behind you, cross the road and then turn right. After a few yards, turn left down Church Street. Pass the church and, where the road bends to the right, go straight ahead along a narrow lane. Just before you reach a house at the end of the lane, climb over a stile on the left. Go straight ahead and cross a second stile at the top of a slope. Continue ahead and, at the far side of the field, cross a drainage ditch. Head diagonally left and carry on to a hedge at the edge of a field. Bear half-left and walk down a slope, before crossing a stile. Keep

a hedge to your right and then walk through a farmyard to a country road.

2 Turn right along the road and right again, ignoring a road off to the left. Pass cottages and keep going until you reach a T-junction. Turn left and, after passing Manor Farm, take the next lane on the right. Follow the lane as it bends to the left, then the right. Where the road ends, go straight ahead on a gravel track. Shortly before reaching buildings ahead of you, go left along a signed footpath. After a few yards, turn right on an unmarked bridleway and keep going until you reach the edge of a wood.

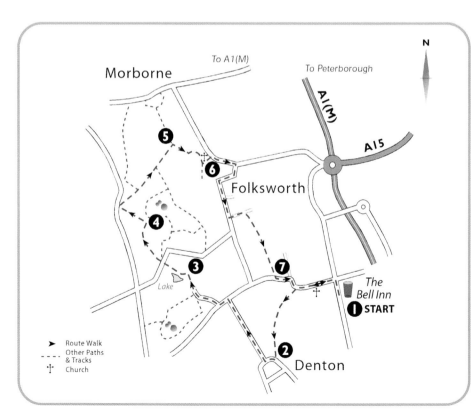

The Anglo-Saxon village of Washingley stood on this site

3 Turn left and then go right, to cross a footbridge spanning a stream. The path takes you to the left, then over another footbridge to the edge of a pretty lake. At a bench beside the lake, bear right and then go over a stile. Walk diagonally left across a grassy field and keep to the main path. As you go through an iron gate, an information board to your right gives details of a small castle which stood here, and which is believed to have been built in either 1066 or the 12th century. Continue to a road in front of you. Turn left then immediately right, to follow a marked bridleway. Further on, an information board on your right describes how the mounds in the adjacent field are all that remain of an Anglo-Saxon village called Washingley. It was abandoned in 1447, and the homes became covered with earth and grass. Further ahead, cross a stream then bear round to the right.

4 At a footbridge, turn left along the bridleway. Just before you reach a road, turn sharp right and pass a barn and radio masts on your left. Further on, pass a marked path to your left and continue until you reach a marker post in front of you. Turn left and cross a ditch, then turn immediately right and continue, keeping a hedge to your right. Walk straight on until you reach another wooden marker post.

5 Turn right here along a grassy track, which later bends to the left and then right. Cross a stile and follow the path round to the left, keeping a hedge to your left. The path soon swings right, taking you past a church. Go through a kissing gate on your left and walk through the churchyard to a road.

6 Turn right along the road and, at a T-junction, turn right again. Follow the main road round to the left. Keep going and then turn left along Townsend Way. After 110 yards, turn right at a signed footpath, then go over a stile and bear half-left across a field. At the far side of the field, go over a stile and continue on a well-trodden path across a grassy field. Drop downhill and cross a stile to arrive at a road.

7 Turn left along the road and continue to a T-junction, where you turn right. Follow the road round to the left and pass the church encountered near the start of the walk. Keep straight ahead and retrace your steps back to the Bell Inn.

Place of Interest
Elton Hall is situated 5 miles north-west of Stilton and is set in beautiful parkland. It houses paintings by Gainsborough, Reynolds and Constable, and the library includes Henry VIII's prayer book. Open through the summer. Telephone: 01832 280468.

Date walk completed:

....

Leighton Bromswold
The Green Man

some short stretches of country lanes to walk along. The route can be appreciated at any time of year, but is perhaps at its best during spring and autumn.

The Green Man is an attractive pub, dating back to around 1600. You will find a friendly and relaxed atmosphere inside the large lounge bar and separate non-smoking dining room. Food is served throughout the pub, and there is a wide choice of dishes – from snacks such as home-made soups through to main meals like sirloin steak in peppercorn sauce, and home-made steak and ale pie. There is also a regularly changing specials board. Nethergate IPA is available, alongside three changing guest ales. A beer garden at the front of the pub can be enjoyed in fine weather.

This enjoyable walk starts in the tiny rural village of Leighton Bromswold. The route takes you through rolling countryside, passing woods and clear brooks. There is an abundance of beautiful scenery to admire along the way and you may see interesting wildlife, such as kestrels and foxes. Most of the paths are well marked and there are

Opening times are 6.30 pm to 11 pm on Tuesday to Thursday, 12 noon to 2.30 pm and 6.30 pm to 11 pm on Friday, 12 noon to 3 pm and 6.30 pm to 11 pm on Saturday, and 12 noon to 3 pm and 7 pm to 10.30 pm on Sunday. Food is available from 7 pm to 9.30 pm on Tuesday to Thursday, 12 noon to 2 pm and 7 pm to 9.30 pm on Friday and Saturday, and 12 noon to 2 pm on Sunday. The pub is closed all day on Monday, and food is not available on Sunday evenings.

Telephone: 01480 890238.

Distance: *4¼ miles*

OS Explorer 225 Huntingdon & St Ives GR 112754

An easy walk over undulating terrain

Starting point: The Green Man's car park. Please seek the landlord's permission to leave your car whilst walking.

How to get there: Leighton Bromswold is situated 9 miles west of Huntingdon, just north of the A14. The pub is located on The Avenue, opposite the public telephone box.

The Walk

1 Leave the front of the pub and turn left. At a curve in the road, bear diagonally left to follow a signed footpath across a field. Continue on the clearly defined path, passing a strip of woodland over to your left. At the far side of a field, head slightly left along an unmarked path over undulating ground. Further on, keep a small strip of woodland immediately to your left and continue ahead. Where the wood ends, walk straight on at a junction of marked tracks, keeping a wire fence to your left. Near the bottom of a slope, go through a wooden gate and bear slightly left through a patch of scrubland. Cross a footbridge over a ditch to arrive at the B660.

2 Cross the road with care and climb a series of wooden steps. Walk ahead along an indistinct path, then veer slightly right to walk up a gentle incline. The ground levels for a while, before dropping downhill. At the far side of a field, you reach a small patch of woodland. Turn right here along an unmarked path,

keeping a wire fence to your left. Further on, a marker arrow on a telegraph pole guides you straight ahead across a field. Walk up a gentle incline and cross a drainage ditch at the far side of a field, then bear slightly left and walk across a field to reach the B660 again.

3 Cross the road and walk ahead along the signed path, keeping a wooden fence and a small wood to your right. Turn right at the end of the fence and walk along a wide grassy bridleway. As you continue with a hedge to your right, there are good views towards the village of Old Weston over to your left. Further on, the bridleway takes you between the lines of two hedgerows. Ignore a marked path to your left, but continue ahead. The bridleway becomes a well-surfaced track, which brings you to a bend in the road. Turn left along the road and walk downhill, where there are good views to the right.

4 At the bottom of the hill, leave the road and turn right to follow a signed path across a field. Veer a little to the left

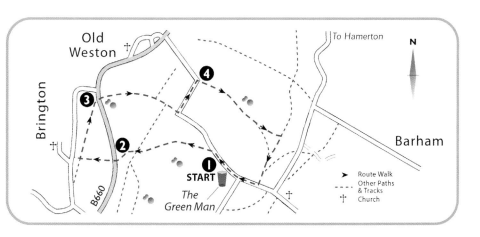

The view near point 4 of the walk

after passing a finger of woodland and go through a gap in the hedge at the edge of a field. Bear slightly left and then walk ahead, keeping a line of trees and a brook to your left. Follow marker arrows as you continue along the side of the brook. Further ahead, a marker arrow guides you to the right along a grassy path. At a gap in a hedge, a yellow arrow on a marker post sends you slightly left and up a gentle slope. At the far side of a field, go over a stile and bear a little to the right. Go over another stile and bear slightly left, then follow marker arrows through a farmyard to arrive at a road. Turn right and you will see the Green Man a short distance ahead of you.

Place of Interest
Hamerton Zoo Park is located 3 miles to the north-east of Leighton Bromswold. Situated in 15 acres of parkland, it was opened as a wildlife conservation sanctuary in 1990 and is now home to over 100 species of beautiful animals from around the world, including meerkats, snakes, birds, gibbons and cheetahs. Open throughout the year. Telephone: 01832 293362.

Date walk completed:

....

The New Sun Inn

This route starts in the historic former market town of Kimbolton, with its magnificent church and beautiful houses. As you walk along High Street, which was the 13th-century market place, you can see Kimbolton Castle and School. The castle, which is owned by the school and still used for studying, is where Queen Katherine of Aragon spent the final twenty months of her life. You then cross the River Kym, before walking through attractive open farmland. There are some fine views from the higher ground, and the spectacular Grafham Water can also be seen along the route.

The New Sun Inn is a 16th-century pub with a lounge bar, conservatory and a separate non-smoking restaurant. Inside there are original beams, real fires in winter and a cosy atmosphere. A patio can be found at the rear of the building. Food is served throughout, and examples include home-made steak and kidney pudding, Dover sole and fillet steak. Sandwiches and light snacks are available at lunchtime and there is also a specials board. Regular ales are Charles Wells Eagle and Bombardier, and Morland Old Speckled Hen.

Distance: *4¼ miles*

OS Explorer 225 Huntingdon & St Ives GR 100677

A moderate walk, with a few gradual inclines

Starting point: The New Sun Inn. A small number of free roadside parking spaces are available opposite the nearby church.

How to get there: Kimbolton is on the B645, 6¼ miles to the north-west of St Neots. The pub is situated on High Street (B645).

Opening times are 11 am to 2.30 pm and 6 pm to 11 pm on Monday to Friday, 11.30 am to 2.30 pm and 6.30 pm to 11 pm on Saturday, and 12 noon to 10.30 pm on Sunday. Food is served from 12 noon to 2.15 pm every day and from 7 pm to 9.30 pm on Tuesday to Saturday (no food on Sunday and Monday evenings).

Telephone: 01480 860052.

The Walk

1 With the pub behind you, turn left along High Street. As you follow the road round to the left, you pass Kimbolton Castle and School to your right. Continue round to the right on the road, then turn left to cross a footbridge over the River Kym. After a few yards, bear slightly right to follow a signed path, heading roughly north-east. At the far side of a field, go diagonally right along an unmarked path. Walk up a gentle incline and aim for the right-hand corner of a wood. At a junction of tracks by the wood, turn left along an unmarked bridleway, keeping trees to your left. Drop downhill and then continue as the path takes you up an incline. The ground levels and you pass a stand of trees on your right, to arrive at a road junction.

2 Turn right then immediately left, and walk along the road. Soon after passing an old farm building on your left, turn right along a well-surfaced bridleway. At a bend in the track, bear diagonally right to follow an unmarked bridleway along a stony path. After 220 yards, bear half-right at a bend in the track and walk across a field. To your left, you can glimpse Grafham Water through the trees. Cross a track at the far side of the field and then bear round to the right. Continue on the unmarked bridleway, keeping trees to your right. At the end of a wood, follow the path as it curves to the right then the left. At the far side of a field, turn left then immediately right. Walk ahead across a field to reach a narrow lane.

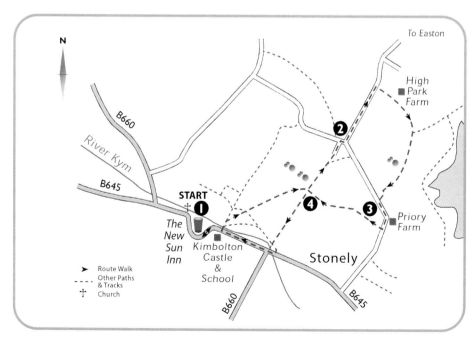

The bridleway at the beginning of the walk

3 Turn left along the lane and follow it as it curves to the right. As you come to Priory Farm, turn right along a signed footpath, keeping a hedge to your right. On reaching a large dead tree in the hedgerow, turn diagonally left along an unmarked path across a field. Walk down a gentle incline and cross a footbridge over a stream, then bear diagonally right and walk uphill. The ground then levels and you reach the junction of tracks by the wood, encountered near the start of the walk.

4 Turn left here and walk downhill, keeping a hedge to your right. As you continue, there are good views ahead and to your left. At the bottom of the hill, bear round to the left and continue along the path to arrive at the B645. Cross the road and then turn right, to cross a road bridge spanning the River Kym. Continue ahead along the pavement and pass Kimbolton Castle and School on your left. Follow the road round to the left and right, then walk ahead to the New Sun Inn, where you will see the church ahead of you.

Place of Interest
Grafham Water is situated 2½ miles to the east of Kimbolton. This 1,500 acre reservoir is one of the largest in England, and can be seen along the route. There is a visitor centre with cycle hire on the east shore, a café, a nature reserve, picnic and play areas. Open all year round. Telephone: 01480 812154.

Date walk completed:

....

55

The Cross Keys

U pwood is a peaceful village set in a beautiful rural landscape. During the Second World War, however, things were a little more hectic. In 1944, 156 Squadron moved here with their Lancaster bombers. They carried out several successful raids over Germany, before leaving in June 1945, and finally disbanding in September 1945. Today, the RAF still has bases in the area. This enjoyable walk takes you through meadows, along country lanes and past mature woodland, with some fine views along the way.

The Cross Keys is a comfortable pub, parts of which are 400 years old. There are two separate bars and a non-smoking restaurant. The cosy lounge bar features low-beamed ceilings and a real fire in winter. Food is served throughout, and there is a regularly changing specials board as well as extensive menus. Each month a themed night features cuisine from a selected country. There are snacks

through to main meals, and examples include home-made soup, ploughman's lunch, grilled sardines and chicken cooked in a white wine, smoked cheese and cream sauce. Regular beers include Adnams Broadside and Bass.

Opening times are 6.30 pm to 11 pm on Monday, 12 noon to 2.30 pm and 6.30 pm to 11 pm on Tuesday to Saturday, and 12 noon to 2.30 pm and 7 pm to 10.30 pm on Sunday. Food is served from 12 noon to 2.30 pm and 6.45 pm to 9 pm on Tuesday to Sunday (no food on Mondays).

Telephone: 01487 813384.

Distance: *4 miles*

OS Explorer 227 Peterborough GR 260828

An easy walk on mainly flat ground

Starting point: The car park at the Cross Keys, but please check with the landlord before leaving your car whilst you walk.

How to get there: Upwood is situated 2 miles south-west of Ramsey, off the B1040. The Cross Keys can be found close to the church.

The Walk

1 Leave the car park and turn left along the road. Pass St Peter's church on your left and continue past an attractive beamed house. Ignore a signed footpath on the right, but carry on to a sharp bend in the road, where you go straight ahead along a signed path. Where the hedge to your left ends, bear half-right and cross a field, then cross a footbridge and bear slightly right again, to cross another field. Go over a stile and bear slightly right. Cross a stile at the end of the field, then continue straight ahead. Go over two stiles in quick succession and then walk on to a road.

2 Turn right along the road and pass through the tiny village of Great Raveley. At a bend in the road, turn right along a signed path. Soon after, go over a stile and turn left. Turn right after a few yards then go over another stile, before heading diagonally left. After passing farm buildings on your left, cross a grassy field, then go over a stile. Turn half-right and, as you pass a wooden marker post next to a stile, bear round to the left. Follow a well-defined path, which takes you along the edge of a wood. As the woodland edge curves away to the left, bear slightly right, aiming for a large oak tree in a hedgerow. Cross a footbridge next to the tree, then bear diagonally left and walk across a field. At the far side of the field, go straight ahead to cross another field. After crossing a footbridge over a ditch, walk straight ahead, aiming for a large tree, which stands at a junction of tracks.

3 Turn right along a signed path and continue between the lines of two hedgerows. Further on, an unmarked path

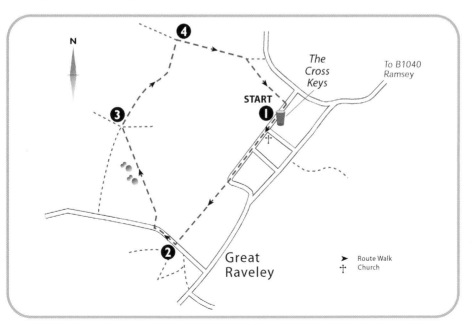

The track on the homeward run

crosses in front of you from left to right. Keep straight ahead here, with a hedge to your right. Continue on the grassy track, where there are good views all around. Eventually, the grassy track becomes a wide gravel path. Follow this as it curves to the left and then continue until you reach a T-junction at the end of the track.

❹ Turn right along the track and, soon after passing a barn to your right, follow a signed path, which takes you diagonally right and up a gentle incline. As you reach the far side of a field, turn left and continue, keeping a wire fence to your right. Further ahead, a marker post guides you to the right then the left, taking you along a path between two houses. At the end of the path you arrive at a road. Turn right along the road and, after 100 yards, you return to the starting point at the pub car park.

Place of Interest

Ramsey Abbey Gatehouse (National Trust) is situated 2½ miles north-east of Upwood, and is part of the remnants of a former Benedictine monastery. The lavishly carved 15th-century gatehouse contains a beautiful oriel window. Telephone: 0870 6095388.

Date walk completed:

....

The Golden Ball

From the starting point at Boxworth, this scenic route winds its way through gently rolling farmland, dotted with tranquil woods and streams. You will be rewarded with some excellent views and along the way you will be able to enjoy picturesque villages such as Knapwell, with its pretty thatched cottages and historic church. Most of the paths are clearly marked, and the walk can be completed in a little under three hours.

The Golden Ball is a 16th-century brick building with a beautiful thatched roof. It has a spacious interior with a large bar and a separate dining area at one end. There is also a beer garden at the rear. Food is served throughout, and there are snacks such as chilli con carne with garlic bread, through to main meals like mignons of fillet steak in filo pastry with whisky and wholegrain mustard sauce. Greene King IPA and Adnams Regatta are available, alongside changing guest beers.

Opening times are 11.30 am to 11 pm on Monday to Saturday and 12 noon to 10.30 pm on Sunday. Food is available from 12 noon to 2.15 pm and 6.30 pm to 9.30 pm on Monday to Thursday, 12 noon to 2.15 pm and 6.30 pm to 10 pm on Friday and Saturday, and 12 noon to 6 pm on Sunday.

Telephone: 01954 267397.

Distance: *6¼ miles*

OS Explorer 225 Huntingdon & St Ives GR 345641

An easy walk, with some gentle slopes

Starting point: The Golden Ball's car park. Please obtain the landlord's permission to leave your car whilst walking.

How to get there: Taking the A14 between Cambridge and Huntingdon, turn off southwards 4½ miles from Cambridge, along an unclassified road to Boxworth. The pub can be found at the far side of the village, on your right.

The Walk

① Leave the car park and turn left along High Street. Soon afterwards, you pass a row of thatched cottages on your right. Beyond a telephone box, follow a signed footpath on your right. After passing through a short stretch of woodland, go through a metal kissing gate and bear slightly right across a grassy field. Go through another gate at the far side of the field, and walk on to a narrow lane, where a beautiful farmhouse faces you. Turn right along the lane and keep straight ahead, passing between two attractive ponds. Follow the path round to the left, keeping the line of a hedge to your left-hand side. The hedge runs out at a corner of a field. At this point, turn right along an unmarked but well-defined path. Further on, pass between two farm buildings and then follow a well-surfaced track up a gentle incline. Continue until you arrive at a crossroads.

② Turn right and walk along a lane. Where the road runs out, go straight ahead on a grassy track. At a marked junction of paths further on, keep straight ahead. Pass under a line of electricity pylons and, as you reach a stretch of woodland in front of you, go over a gate and continue with the wood to your right. Veer slightly left as you cross a field and then go through a wooden gate at the edge of a farm. Walk on to a gravel track, then turn right along the track and continue as it twist and turns. At a marker post in a hedgerow, turn left and walk along the edge of a field, keeping a hedge to your left. At the end of the field, walk through a gap in the hedge ahead of you and pass a marker post, before continuing straight on. Keep going until you arrive at a narrow lane.

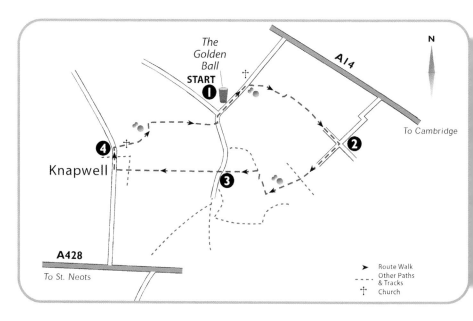

60

This attractive pond is passed near the start of the walk

❸ Cross the lane and follow the marked path on the opposite side. After passing a stretch of woodland on your right, the path drops downhill slightly. At a junction of paths, go straight ahead and cross a footbridge over a stream, before walking on to a narrow road. Turn right along the road and pass through the pretty village of Knapwell. Ignore marked paths to the right and left, but continue until you come to a left-hand bend in the road.

❹ Turn right here along a signed path. Soon, you pass All Saints' church, with its fine 14th-century tower. Cross a footbridge over a stream and then follow a well-trodden path over a grassy field, keeping a wood to your right. The path curves to the left, before taking you along the edge of a wood on your left-hand side. At the far edge of the wood, turn right and walk up a gentle slope, keeping a fence to your left. Cross a farm track and then continue straight ahead, with a hedge to your right. At the end of the field, go right through a gap in the hedge, then turn immediately left and go through an iron kissing gate ahead of you. Turn left along a road and follow it round to the right, where you will see the Golden Ball in front of you.

Places of Interest
Wimpole Hall and **Wimpole Home Farm** (both National Trust) are situated 7½ miles to the south. The hall is a magnificent 18th-century building set in an extensive wooded park, while the farm is home to rare animal breeds. Telephone: 01223 206000.

Date walk completed:

....

61

The Royal Oak

Situated 6 miles south-west of Cambridge, the beautiful village of Barrington is centred around a sprawling green, complete with its own cricket pitch. This circuit takes you through rolling wooded countryside, where there are some excellent views to be enjoyed. A relatively short walk, which can be completed in about two hours, the route would be an ideal choice for families, or for those with a busy schedule.

The Royal Oak is an impressive timbered building with a large thatched roof, and enjoys a quiet position overlooking the village green. Inside there are two bars and a comfortable non-smoking restaurant. The wide choice of food available includes hot and cold bar snacks such as turkey and cranberry sandwiches, chicken Kiev and fish and chips, while the

restaurant offers treats like fillet of beef. There is always a fish of the day and a carvery on Sundays. Greene King IPA is served, and is supplemented with guest ales from a variety of brewers, including Nethergate, Elgood's, Adnams and Potton.

Opening times are 12 noon to 2.30 pm and 5 pm to 11 pm on Monday to Friday, 12 noon to 11 pm on Saturday, and 12 noon to 10.30 pm on Sunday. Food is served from 12 noon to 2 pm and 6.30 pm to 9.30 pm on Monday to Friday, 12 noon to 2.30 pm and 6 pm to 9.30 pm on Saturday, and from 12 noon to 4 pm and 6.30 pm to 9 pm on Sunday.

Telephone: 01223 870791.

Distance: 3¾ miles

OS Explorer 209 Cambridge GR 390494

An easy walk, with one gentle incline

Starting point: The Royal Oak's car park. Please obtain the landlord's permission to leave your car whilst walking.

How to get there: Take the A10 between Royston and junction 10 of the M11. Turn off westwards, 4 miles from Royston, and pass through Shepreth. Cross the River Cam and then follow the road round to the right. Soon you will see the pub on your right, opposite the village green.

The Walk

① With the pub behind you, turn right and walk along the pavement. Pass the village green/cricket pitch on your left and, at the end of the green, turn left along a well-surfaced lane. Pass a pretty thatched cottage on your right and then bear round to the right, where the lane becomes a muddy bridleway. Immediately after passing a white house on your right, turn left and go through a kissing gate, to follow a signed path. Continue straight ahead, keeping a hedge to your right. At the end of a stretch of woodland, ignore an unmarked path to your right, but keep straight ahead. Where the hedge to your right ends, walk straight on, this time with a hedge to your left. After passing a farmhouse, you arrive at a gravel track.

② Turn right along the track and then turn immediately left, to follow a signed path. Walk up a gentle incline, keeping a drainage ditch to your left. As you reach a strip of woodland in front of you, turn right. At the end of the tree-line, turn left and continue up an incline. Look behind you for some far-reaching views across the countryside. Soon after, the ground levels out, bringing you to a junction of paths by a strip of woodland. Turn left here and walk along the edge of a field, keeping the trees to your right. At the far side of the field, a marker arrow guides you straight ahead along a track through woodland. Go over a stile at the far side of the wood, to arrive at an unmarked grassy track.

③ Turn left along the track and continue down a gentle incline, keeping trees and a hedge to your left. At the bottom of the slope you reach a gravel track, where a narrow road can be seen to your right.

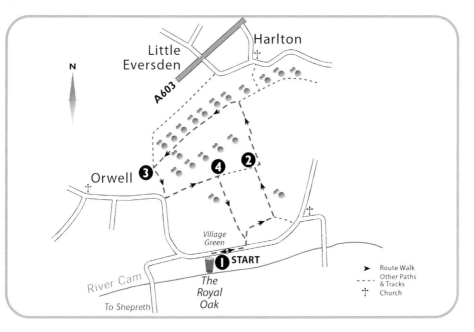

A wide open view near point 3 of the walk

Turn left along the track, to follow a signed public footpath. After about 300 yards, you reach a marker post on your left-hand side.

4 Turn right here and walk straight ahead across a field. At the far side of the field, follow another marker post, which guides you straight on. Continue, keeping a hedge to your right. At the end of the field, walk straight ahead along a tree-lined path. At an unmarked fork in the path bear slightly right and then continue straight ahead. Further on you emerge at the edge of the village green, with a cricket pavilion to your left. Bear diagonally left and walk across the edge of the green, then bear right along the well-surfaced lane used earlier. Turn right along the road and continue back to the Royal Oak.

Date walk completed:

....

Places of Interest

Shepreth Wildlife Park is situated a mile to the south of Barrington, with large lakes set in natural grounds. There is a lot to see, including monkeys, tigers, fish and reptiles. Telephone: 09066 800031.

Fowlmere RSPB Nature Reserve is located 2½ miles south-east of Barrington. A wide range of wild birds can be seen throughout the year and there are several comfortable hides from which to watch them. Telephone: 01763 208978.

The Pheasant

The idyllic village of Great Chishill is the starting point for this walk. Formerly in the neighbouring county of Essex, it was transferred for administration purposes to Cambridge-shire in 1895. This area is said to be the highest in the county, and the footpaths at the beginning and end of the route offer sweeping views north towards Cambridge and beyond. You will also get a tantalising taste of the Icknield Way – one of the oldest roads in Britain, and one of

the few long-distance paths to have existed before Roman times.

The Pheasant is an attractive inn, with a large beer garden at the rear. Inside, the low ceilings, beamed walls and real fire in winter enhance the warm and friendly atmosphere. Meals are served in the bar, where there is also a non-smoking eating area. The varied menu includes snacks such as smoked salmon and horseradish sandwich, through to main meals like chicken breast in Parma ham, or wild mushroom lasagne. Greene King IPA is available, alongside changing guest ales.

Opening times are 12 noon to 3 pm and 6 pm to 11 pm on Monday to Friday, 12 noon to 11 pm on Saturday, and 12 noon to 10.30 pm on Sunday. Food is served from 12 noon to 2 pm and 6 pm to 9 pm throughout the week.

Telephone: 01763 838535.

Distance: 5 miles

OS Explorers 209 Cambridge and 194 Hertford & Bishop's Stortford
GR 423388

An easy walk, with a gradual incline towards the end

Starting point: The Pheasant's car park. Please check with the landlord before leaving your car while you walk.

How to get there: From Royston, head east on the B1039. In the village of Barley, go left on the B1039. Pass Chishill Windmill on the right, then turn left into Heydon Road. The Pheasant is on your right, beyond the public telephone box.

The Walk

1 From the front of the pub, cross the road and turn right to walk along the pavement. Pass New Road on your left, then, a little further ahead, turn left at a signed footpath. Follow this down a gentle slope, before passing an orchard on your right. Soon afterwards, ignore an unmarked path off to your left, but continue straight ahead. The path curves to the right as you pass open fields on your left. Drop downhill and head towards farm buildings. As you approach them, there are good views ahead of you. At the edge of the farm, turn left along a gravel track and then turn right after 50 yards, passing cottages on your left-hand side. Walk straight on, keeping to the clearly defined path. After dropping downhill, you arrive at a junction of tracks.

2 Turn right and walk along the historic Icknield Way, from where there are good views across the farmland to your right. Kestrels can sometimes be seen hovering overhead here, as they search for food in the fields below. Continue between the lines of two hedges, before passing the perimeter of a golf course to your left. Soon after, you reach a footpath marker post ahead of you.

3 Turn right here and walk along a straight grassy path. In summer the wild flowers along the edge attract butterflies and other insects. Soon you walk up a gentle incline. Look back here for some fine views. Continue through a lightly wooded area to arrive at a road.

4 Turn right and walk along the pavement, passing through the village of

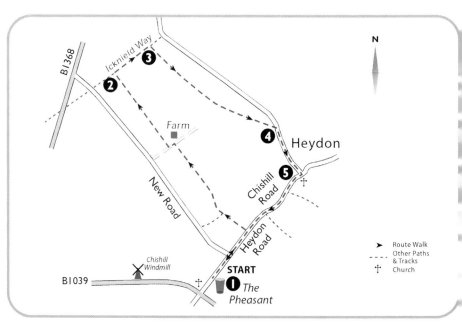

Wide skies along the Icknield Way

Heydon, with its attractive houses. Just beyond a public telephone box on your right-hand side, you reach a T-junction.

5 Turn right along Chishill Road and pass the pretty church on your left. Carry on past the King William IV pub and, where the pavement runs out, keep straight ahead along the road, taking care to look for any oncoming traffic. Further on, you pass picturesque thatched cottages with beautiful flower gardens. Continue past the marked footpath that was used near the start of the route, and you arrive back at the Pheasant.

Date walk completed:

....

Place of Interest

Chishill Windmill is situated just off the B1039, a short distance west of the village. It was built in 1819, using timbers from an earlier mill. There is a small adjacent picnic area.

The Pear Tree

With the clear water of the River Granta running through its centre, the historic village of Hildersham provides an attractive setting for the start of this walk. Its name derives from the word 'Hilderic', which is an Anglo-Saxon personal name. It also holds the curious distinction of being the last parish in England in which the strip-fields system was abolished. There are some fine views to be enjoyed along the way, as well as the chance to walk along the route of an ancient Roman road.

The Pear Tree pub has a single bar with a stone floor, and offers good quality food in a friendly and relaxed atmosphere. There is a daily-changing specials board as well as the main menu. The ploughman's lunches are particularly recommended, perhaps accompanied by a pint of Greene King IPA, Abbot Ale or one of the occasional guest beers. Behind the attractive building is a small beer garden.

Opening times are 11.45 am to 2 pm and 6.30 pm to 11 pm on Monday to Saturday, and 12 noon to 2 pm and 7 pm to 10.30 pm on Sunday. Food is available from 11.45 am to 2 pm and 6.30 pm to 9.30 pm on Monday to Saturday, and 12 noon to 2 pm and 7 pm to 9 pm on Sunday.

Telephone: 01223 891680.

Distance: *6¼ miles*

OS Explorer 209 Cambridge
GR 543484

A moderate walk, with gradual inclines

Starting point: The Pear Tree's car park. Please ask permission before leaving your car while you walk.

How to get there: Hildersham is 7½ miles south-east of Cambridge, just off the A1307. The pub stands opposite the village green.

The Walk

1 Leave the pub and turn left along the road. Shortly before reaching the River Granta, turn right and go through a wooden gate next to a footpath sign. Aim for another wooden gate ahead of you, and then follow the path as it curves slightly to the right, taking you close to the river. As you reach a footbridge on your left, go diagonally right and walk across a grassy field. Go through a wooden kissing gate and then turn right along a well-surfaced track. After about 275 yards, take an unmarked path on your left, where you pass trees to your left

and a wooden fence to your right. Walk straight ahead along the edge of a field. Shortly before reaching a line of electricity pylons, the path curves to the right, then the left. Continue straight ahead, passing underneath the pylons. Soon after, you reach a junction of paths.

2 Turn left here and, further on, cross a footbridge over the river. Keep straight ahead and cross a smaller bridge spanning a ditch. Walk straight on until you come to a country road. Turn right along the road, keeping alert to any oncoming traffic. After 660 yards, take the signed bridleway on your left and follow it up a

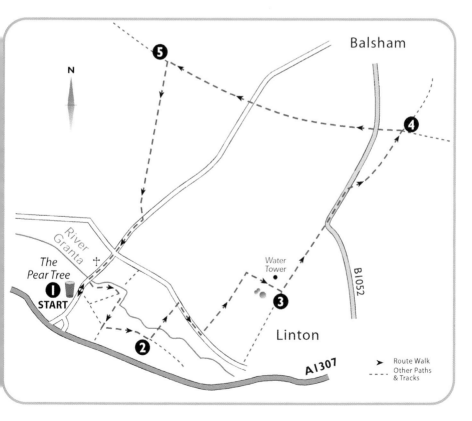

gentle incline. Pass the edge of a wood on your left and continue up the slope. On the brow of the hill, you can catch your breath and enjoy some fantastic views, from the comfort of a wooden bench. Turn right by the bench and follow the path, which eventually takes you past an imposing water tower, and on to a junction of paths.

Near the start of the walk

❸ Turn left here and walk along a gravel path, passing the water tower on your left-hand side. After walking down a gentle slope, you arrive at a road. Go straight ahead, passing Chilford Hall Vineyard on the left. Take the next signed path on your right. Cross a field and aim for a marker post in a hedgerow. Once here, go straight across a field and continue to a junction of tracks.

❹ Turn left to follow the course of a Roman road. A little further on, cross the B1052 and pick up the path again on the opposite side. Continue between two hedgerows, where in late summer and early autumn there is an abundance of blackberries and elderberries. Keep to the main path and then cross a narrow road

further ahead. Follow the path on the opposite side and keep going until you reach a wooden marker post on your left.

❺ Turn left here and follow a grassy path, from where there are good views to the left and right. Walk straight ahead until you arrive at a road. Turn right and continue with caution. At a crossroads, go straight ahead, passing pretty houses along the way. Cross a bridge over the river and then carry on until you return to the Pear Tree pub on your right.

Date walk completed:

....

Place of Interest

The **Imperial War Museum** is at Duxford, 5 miles south-west of the village, close to junction 10 of the M11. This is Europe's premier aviation museum, which also houses military vehicles and naval exhibits. Regular flying displays also take place. Telephone: 01223 835000.

The Ancient Shepherds

T he picturesque village of Fen Ditton marks the start of this enjoyable walk. Although it is located only 2 miles from Cambridge city centre, its thatched cottages, elegant church and half-timbered houses lend a truly rural atmosphere to the setting. After leaving behind the quiet village streets, the route takes you beside a peaceful stretch of the River Cam, where a variety of water birds are disturbed only by the occasional chugging sound of a passing narrowboat. The walk continues through open farmland and the pretty village of Horningsea, before returning you to the riverbank, and on to complete the route.

The Ancient Shepherds is an attractive building, with whitewashed walls and a pleasant garden to the rear. Built in 1540, it was originally three cottages. Inside there are low-beamed ceilings and inglenook fireplaces. The lounge has comfortable leather Chesterfield seats, complementing the relaxed atmosphere. Meals are served in the bars or in the non-smoking restaurant. There is a good choice of food, from lighter snacks such as baguettes and sausages and mash, to duck in orange sauce or chicken with asparagus. There are also daily changing fish specials. Ales are Adnams Bitter and Greene King IPA.

Distance: 5½ miles

OS Explorers 209 Cambridge and 226 Ely & Newmarket
GR 485602

An easy walk on flat ground

Starting point: The car park at the Ancient Shepherds. Please obtain the landlord's permission to leave your car whilst walking.

How to get there: From the A14 north of Cambridge, take the B1047 signed to Cambridge and the airport. After ½ mile, turn right along High Street. The Ancient Shepherds is immediately on the left.

Opening times are 12 noon to 3 pm and 6 pm to 11 pm on Monday to Thursday, 11 am to 3 pm and 6.30 pm to 11 pm on Friday and Saturday, and 12 noon to 5 pm on Sunday. Lunch is served every day from 12 noon to 2 pm, and evening meals on Monday to Saturday from 6.30 pm to 9 pm.

Telephone: 01223 293280.

The Walk

1 Leaving the front of the pub, turn left down High Street, then go right along Church Street, passing St Mary's church. Follow the road as it bends to the left, then the right. Pass the Plough pub on your left, then go straight ahead. Where the road runs out, follow a signed path across a grassy field. Go through a kissing gate by a stone cottage, then follow the path beside the river. Look out for herons fishing by the bank here. Continue under a bridge, with the A14 above you. Further ahead, go left at a marker post and walk between two houses. At Baits Bite Lock, cross the river via two footbridges.

2 On the far side of the river, turn right and walk along a well-surfaced track. A little further on, the track becomes a gravel path; it gets more muddy as you continue. In spring and summer, a variety of water birds breed by the grassy banks along this stretch of water. Continue straight on, where there are fine views along the river. Immediately before reaching a bridge at Clayhithe, follow the path to the left, which brings you to a narrow road.

3 Cross the road with care, then turn right to cross the bridge over the river. On the far side of the bridge turn left along a

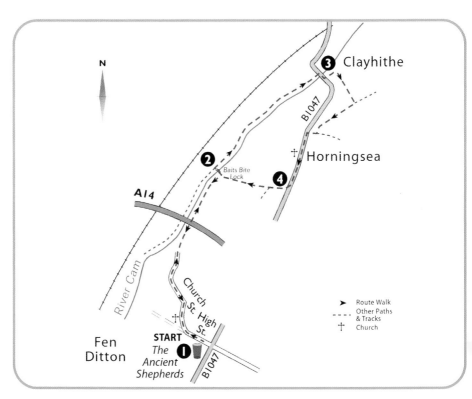

signed footpath. Immediately after passing a large house, bear right on a stony track. The path twists and turns, before taking you between two farm buildings. After 220 yards, turn right at a marker post and walk across a field. Pass a large, lone tree and continue straight ahead where an unmarked path goes off to the left. A little further on, the track bends to the right. At this point, go over a stile in front of you, then go diagonally right across a field, to cross a second stile. On your right you pass Eye Hall Farm. Go through a kissing gate and continue straight ahead on the path. After 330 yards, turn right along a gravel track, which brings you to a road. Cross with caution, then go left along a grass verge, which gives way to a pavement as you enter Horningsea. In spring, the village echoes to the sound of a rookery, which you pass on your left-hand side. Keep going straight on, and pass the Plough and Fleece pub on your right. After 330 yards, you come to a signed footpath.

Baits Bite Lock by the River Cam

❹ Turn right here, then continue straight ahead. Cross a small footbridge spanning a drainage ditch. Follow the path as it bends slightly to the left, then cross another footbridge over a narrow stream. Turn left and walk away from Baits Bite Lock, on the path encountered near the start of this route. Continue along the riverbank and under the A14 bridge. Pass the stone cottage seen earlier on the walk and carry on to the road. Once here, retrace your steps through the village, past the church and back to the start.

Date walk completed:

....

Places of Interest
Cambridge city centre has a host of attractions, not least its world-famous university colleges.
Anglesey Abbey, Gardens & Lode Mill (National Trust) are located 4 miles north-east of Fen Ditton. Dating from 1600, the house contains a wonderful collection of paintings, furniture, silver, tapestries and clocks. The garden has year-round floral interest. Telephone: 01223 810080.

Reach
The Dyke's End

Nowadays, it is hard to imagine that the peaceful village of Reach was once a busy port. Goods, including building materials, were transported by boat along Reach Lode to the River Cam and, from there, were taken onwards to surrounding towns and cities. Lodes are short stretches of water, which were designed both for drainage and navigation. Most are very straight and almost all date back to Roman times. Today they are used by pleasure craft. Two such lodes – Reach and Burwell – feature prominently in this scenic and satisfying circuit.

The Dyke's End is an attractive village pub dating back to the 18th century. Inside there is a single bar and two separate non-smoking dining rooms. Candlelight, a ticking clock and, in winter, a real fire lend a relaxed atmosphere to the simple, yet elegant surroundings. You can eat anywhere in the pub and seasonally changing menus offer a fine selection of quality home-made food, from lunchtime snacks like chef's steak sandwich with hollandaise butter, to main dishes such as faggots with mash and onion gravy, or grilled goats cheese and warm salad of Spanish vegetables. An impressive selection of well-kept ales include Woodforde's Wherry, Greene King IPA and various beers from Archers brewery. Aspall's Cyder is also available.

Opening times are 6 pm to 11 pm on Monday, 12 noon to 2.30 pm and 6 pm to 11 pm on Tuesday to Saturday, and 12 noon to 3 pm and 7 pm to 10.30 pm on Sunday. Food is served from 12 noon to 2 pm and 7 pm to 9 pm on Tuesday to Saturday, and from 12 noon to 3 pm on Sunday (no food served on Monday or Sunday evenings).

Telephone: 01638 743816.

Distance: *6¾ miles*

OS Explorer 226 Ely & Newmarket
GR 567662

A moderate walk on mainly flat ground; muddy in places

Starting point: The car park at the Dyke's End. Please seek the landlord's permission to leave your car whilst walking.

How to get there: From Newmarket, head towards Burwell on the B1103 and then turn left along the B1102. After ½ mile turn right on an unclassified road. Continue to Reach and you will see the pub overlooking the village green.

The Walk

1 With the pub behind you, cross over to the far side of the village green. As you reach Hill Farm, turn right along the road and pass a telephone box on your right. At a bend in the road, walk straight ahead along a narrow lane called The Hythe. At the end of the lane, go left to cross a footbridge spanning Reach Lode, then turn right along a track. After 90 yards, leave the track by branching off to the right and then cross a stile to follow a grassy path, keeping the water to your right. After passing underneath a line of electricity pylons, go over a stile and keep straight ahead on the path. As you continue along the raised bank, there are excellent views across the countryside. Further along the track, Burwell Lode joins Reach Lode from the right. Continue and then cross a stile to arrive at a narrow road.

2 Turn right along the road and cross a bridge over the lode. Turn right on the far side of the bridge to follow a signed path. Pass cottages on your left and then keep straight ahead. Further on, cross a wooden footbridge. To the left you will see a path running beside Wicken Lode, which leads to Wicken Fen Nature Reserve. Ignore this (unless you want to explore the reserve), but go over a stile in front of you and continue straight on. As you pass the perimeter of the reserve to your left, look out for interesting birds and other wildlife. Further ahead, you will see Reach Lode to the right. Continue as the path bears slightly left, taking you beside Burwell Lode. Cross a stile and keep straight ahead. Carry on until you reach a footbridge.

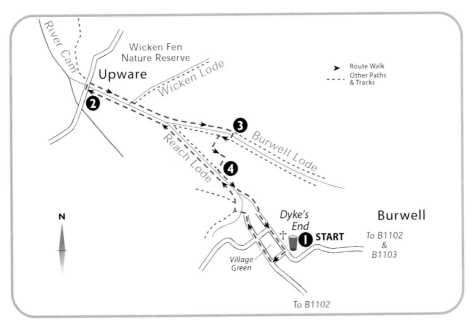

Looking along Reach Lode, near Wicken Fen

3 Cross the bridge and, on the other side, turn right. After 150 yards you come to a wooden kissing gate. At this point, turn left and descend the grassy bank, then go straight ahead on an unmarked, but clearly defined track. At the end of the track, go through a kissing gate and turn left. Go through another kissing gate and pass barns on your right. Soon after, turn right and go through a kissing gate. Continue straight ahead on a clearly defined grassy track. At the end of the track, go through a kissing gate and then climb a grassy bank, where you arrive at Reach Lode.

4 Turn left and walk along the path, keeping the water to your right. Pass a disused building on your left and then continue under a line of electricity pylons.

At the end of Reach Lode, you meet two metal kissing gates. Go through the one on the right and continue to a narrow road. Keep going straight ahead along the road and, after passing a church on your left, you arrive back at the pub.

Place of Interest
Wicken Fen Nature Reserve (National Trust) is a haven for birds, plants, insects and mammals. It is situated 2½ miles to the north-west of Reach and is accessible on foot from point 2 of this route. Telephone: 01353 720274.

Date walk completed:

....

The Anchor Inn

S utton Gault is situated on the western edge of the Isle of Ely, which at one time stood with its ancient cathedral surrounded by water. Since the draining of the fens, however, flooding has been controlled, and now rich agricultural land stands in place of large tracts of swamp. This attractive walk takes you beside the New Bedford River – also known as the Hundred Foot Drain – which was built for the Duke of Bedford by Dutch drainage experts in around 1650. After a short stretch of road, you walk back along the banks of the Old Bedford River, which was built in around 1630, before another stretch of road returns you to the start.

The Anchor Inn was built in 1650 and benefits from a beautiful riverside location. The single bar has four adjacent rooms with beamed ceilings, scrubbed pine tables, real fires in winter and traditional gaslight. Outside there is a terrace overlooking the river. The regularly changing menus offer a wide choice of quality food, including dishes such as braised oxtail with roast root vegetables, local sausages and mash with red wine gravy and ginger and marmalade sponge pudding with fresh custard. Ales are served straight from the cask and include Hobson's Choice and Boathouse Bitter, from City of Cambridge Brewery.

Opening times are 12 noon to 3.30 pm and 7 pm to 11 pm on Monday to Friday, 12 noon to 3.30 pm and 6.30 pm to 11 pm on Saturday, and 12 noon to 3.30 pm and 7 pm to 10.30 pm on Sunday. Food is served every day from 12 noon to 2 pm and 7 pm to 9 pm (Saturday evening meals are from 6.30 pm to 9.30 pm).

Telephone: 01353 778537.

Distance: *8 miles*

OS Explorer 225 Huntingdon & St Ives GR 428796

A moderate walk on flat ground

Starting point: The Anchor Inn's car park. Please check with the landlord before leaving your car whilst you walk.

How to get there: From the A142 between Ely and Chatteris, turn off south-west 3½ miles from Ely, along the B1381. After passing through Sutton, turn right along an unclassified road. The inn is on your left just before you reach the river.

The Walk

1 From the entrance of the pub, turn left and then left again as you reach the riverbank. Walk away from the pub, keeping the New Bedford River, or Hundred Foot Drain, to your right. Soon after, go over a stile beside a wooden gate and continue straight ahead. After about 600 yards, both the path and the river curve to the right slightly. As you walk along the raised embankment, there are clear views for miles around. To the right you can see the raised banks of the Old Bedford River, and in between are the Hundred Foot Washes. These fertile pastures are grazed by cattle, but for part of the winter controlled flooding means that the land is under water. This in turn attracts large numbers of wildfowl to the area. Further along, the road to your left comes close to the path. At this point, go over a stile and then continue straight ahead. Swans, herons and other birds can be encountered here. Walk on and cross a stile at the edge of a main road.

2 Turn right along the road and cross a bridge spanning the river. Continue along the road with care. You may wish to cross over occasionally, in order to keep a clear line of sight towards any oncoming traffic. A little further on, cross a road bridge over the Old Bedford River and continue for a short distance, until you arrive at a footpath sign on your right-hand side.

3 Go over a stile next to the sign and continue straight on, keeping the river to your right. After passing a house on your left, go over a stile and then keep straight ahead, where the path becomes slightly wider. Again, there are good views over

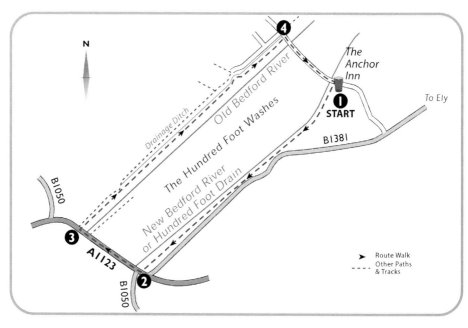

The New Bedford River

the surrounding countryside. Further ahead, a narrow drainage ditch can be seen to the left. Go over a stile by a wooden gate and continue straight ahead. As you reach a pair of bridges on either side of you, go over two stiles in quick succession, then continue straight ahead along the raised embankment. The path later curves sharply to the left and right, before continuing in a straight line once more. Immediately before you come to a road, step off the grassy path onto a well-surfaced track. Continue straight on for a few yards, then cross a stile at the edge of a minor road.

❹ Turn right along the road and continue with caution. On the opposite side of the road is a raised wooden walkway, which you may wish to use. Cross a bridge over the Old Bedford River

then, a little further on, cross a bridge over the New Bedford River, which brings you back to the Anchor Inn where the walk began.

Places of Interest

The historic city of **Ely**, 7½ miles to the east of Sutton Gault, is well worth a visit. Two notable attractions are the magnificent Norman cathedral, and the house where Oliver Cromwell and his family lived between 1636 and 1647 (also home to the Tourist Information Centre). Telephone: 01353 662062.

Date walk completed:

....

The Oliver Twist

This walk starts from the tiny village of Guyhirn, which is located just a few miles away from the Lincolnshire county border. The linear route – the only one in this book – takes you south-west along the Nene Way for 3½ miles, beside Morton's Leam, and then leads you back the same way, with a second chance to enjoy this pretty stretch of water. Constructed in the 15th century, the leam leaves the River Nene at Guyhirn and runs for 13 miles before rejoining the river at Peterborough. It forms part of the complex fenland drainage system and is an attractive feature for both walkers and wildlife alike.

The Oliver Twist is a welcoming village pub with one large lounge bar. A wide variety of food is on offer, ranging from snacks such as soup and baguettes, through to more substantial meals like medallions of lamb and chateaubriand. On Sundays, traditional roasts are served. Tetley's Imperial is the regular ale and is accompanied by regularly changing guest beers. Elgood's Black Dog Mild is also usually available.

Opening times are 11.30 am to 2.30 pm and 6 pm to 11 pm on Monday to Saturday, and 12 noon to 2.30 pm and 6 pm to 10.30 pm on Sunday. Food is served from 11.30 am to 2 pm and 6 pm to 10 pm on Monday to Saturday, and from 12 noon to 2 pm and 6 pm to 9 pm on Sunday.

Telephone: 01945 450523.

Distance: *7 miles*

OS Explorer 235 Wisbech & Peterborough North
GR 397031

An easy walk on flat terrain

Starting point: The Oliver Twist's car park. Please check with the landlord before leaving your car whilst walking.

How to get there: Guyhirn is situated 4 miles north of March, just off the A47. The Oliver Twist is on High Road.

The Walk

❶ Turn right out of the car park and, at a bend in the road, cross over and climb some steps. At the top of the steps, cross the main road with care and turn left. Go over a road bridge, where the River Nene and Morton's Leam can be seen to the right. Continue to a traffic island and cross a stile on your right, to follow a path marked 'Nene Way'. After passing a building on your left, ignore an unmarked path to your right, but go through a gap in the hedge in front of you. Continue ahead, then follow the path as it bends to the right, along a raised bank. Keep going along the path and cross a stile further ahead. Walk straight on, keeping Morton's Leam to your right. Further on, you pass a wooded area over to your left, and there are good views to your right, where the raised banks of the River Nene

can be seen. In winter, the fields between the two stretches of water sometimes become flooded, attracting wildfowl. Further on, you reach a third stile.

❷ Cross the stile and continue straight ahead along the raised grassy bank. Further ahead, go over another stile and then continue in the same direction, where there are some fine views to your left and right. Cross a fifth stile further on, where a marker arrow guides you straight ahead. The fields to the right of the leam are a good place to see birds of prey hunting, particularly throughout autumn and winter. Go over another stile further ahead and walk straight on. Over to your left you can see a drainage ditch, which runs parallel with the path. Walk on until you reach a seventh stile, where a bridge and farm buildings can be seen over to the right.

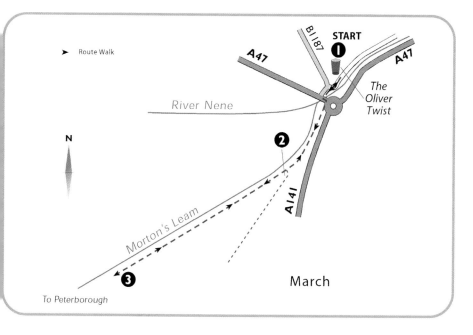

Looking back along the path, Morton's Leam is on the left

❸ This stile marks the halfway point of the route. Do not cross the stile, but turn around and retrace your steps, this time with Morton's Leam on your left-hand side. Continue back along the raised grassy bank, where you can now enjoy the views that were behind you on the first half of the journey. Continue straight ahead, crossing the stiles encountered earlier. As you near the end of the walk, the path curves to the left and takes you back towards the traffic island. Cross the stile beside the island to leave the Nene Way. Turn left and walk back along the pavement beside the main road. Go over the bridge used earlier and then cross the main road to descend the steps. Turn right and return to the pub.

Place of Interest

Wisbech & Fenland Museum is located at Wisbech, 4½ miles north-east of Guyhirn. There are displays illustrating the changing landscape of the fens, as well as local maps and photographs, coins, medals, artworks and natural history exhibits. The museum also holds the original manuscript of Charles Dickens' *Great Expectations*, which can be viewed on the first Saturday of each month. Telephone: 01945 583817

Date walk completed:

....

The Fox and Hounds

Exton is a peaceful hamlet with honey-coloured stone cottages clustered around a village green. Mentioned in the Domesday survey, its name means 'ox farm'. This walk features gently rolling farmland, woodland and two beautiful lakes, which are set in the grounds of Exton Park – a magnificent privately owned country estate, which has been home to the Noel family (the Earls of Gainsborough) for almost 400 years. There are some fine views to be enjoyed along the way, together with an air of tranquillity.

The Fox and Hounds is a warm and friendly 17th-century coaching inn, overlooking the village green. The comfortable interior comprises a public bar, lounge and separate dining area, with food also served in the two bars. In winter, real fires roar, while a garden can be enjoyed on warmer days. The varied menu includes jacket potatoes, soup, home-made Italian pizza, pan-fried calves' liver with bacon and mash, and grilled halibut. Greene King IPA is always available, together with guest ales from local brewer Grainstore, or Elgood's of Cambridgeshire.

Opening times are 11 am to 2.30 pm and 6 pm to 11 pm on Monday to Saturday, and 12 noon to 3 pm and 7 pm to 10.30 pm on Sunday. Food is served from 12 noon to 2 pm and 7 pm to 9 pm on Monday to Friday, 12 noon to 2.15 pm and 6.30 pm to 9.15 pm on Saturday, and 12 noon to 2.15 pm and 7 pm to 9 pm on Sunday.

Telephone: 01572 812403.

Distance: *5¼ miles*

OS Explorer 234 Rutland Water GR 925112

An easy walk, mainly flat with some gentle inclines

Starting point: The car park of the Fox and Hounds. Please seek the landlord's permission to leave your car whilst walking.

How to get there: Turn off the A606 between Oakham and Stamford, heading north on a minor road, 4 miles from Oakham and just west of Whitwell. After 1½ miles, the village green is reached, where the pub can be seen to your right.

The Walk

1 With the main entrance of the pub behind you, turn left, then immediately right. At the end of the village green, go straight ahead on High Street. At a T-junction, go left, and then follow the road round to the right along West End. Pass a farm building on the left, then bear left. After crossing a cattle grid, turn right along a signed path. Pass a stretch of woodland on the left and continue to a junction of paths. Turn right along a signed bridleway, which at this point is a well-surfaced farm lane. Walk on to a sharp right-hand bend.

2 At this point, turn left on a marked path. As you reach a sharp bend, go over a stile and cross a field. Go over a stile at the far side of the field, then follow the track straight ahead, passing a wood on the left. The track takes you up a gentle incline, before the ground levels out. Take the next marked path on the right, which leads you across a field. Ignore a footpath off to the left, but continue straight on, eventually passing woodland on your left. The path takes you down a gentle slope to a junction with a narrow estate road. Go straight on, as you continue to drop downhill, passing through woodland as you walk.

3 At the bottom of the hill, turn right at a footpath and descend a series of steep

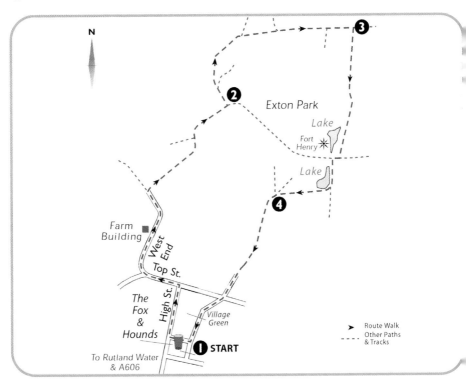

The lake, with Fort Henry just visible in the background

wooden steps. Follow the path through woodland, where a narrow stream accompanies you to your right. The path bends right, revealing a beautiful lake with an intriguing folly, known as Fort Henry. It was built in 1788 by William Legg, for Henry, Earl of Gainsborough. After passing close to the lake, the path then veers away slightly, taking you up a gentle incline beside the edge of a field. At the end of the lake, turn right along an estate road and, after a few yards, go over a stile on the left. Pass a smaller lake on the right, to arrive at an estate lane. Bear half-right, then follow the signed footpath on the right, keeping the lake on your right-hand side. Go over a stile and walk straight ahead, up a gentle slope. The ground steepens and you reach a junction of tracks.

4 Bear left, keeping to the well-surfaced lane, which is marked as a bridleway. The path continues to climb, before curving to the right. After the ground levels, cross a cattle grid and walk along a residential road. At a road junction, go straight ahead, passing pretty thatched cottages on the right. The Fox and Hounds is soon visible ahead of you.

Date walk completed:

....

Places of Interest
Rutland Falconry and Owl Centre is about a mile south-west of the village. As well as regular flying displays, there is a chance to get close to birds of prey. Telephone: 07778 152814.
Rutland Railway Museum is 3 miles north-west of Exton. This railway heritage centre has steam and diesel engines, and is open mainly at weekends. Telephone: 01572 813203.

Upper Hambleton
The Finch's Arms

1976, however, Lower Hambleton was flooded when Rutland Water was created, leaving just Upper Hambleton and Middle Hambleton, now known locally just as Hambleton. The area is believed to have once been the regional capital of the Anglo-Saxon kings, but today, visitors are attracted simply by the beautiful landscape, and the many leisure activities on offer.

This walk starts in the tiny village of Upper Hambleton, and takes you round a circuit of the peninsula jutting out into Rutland Water – western Europe's largest man-made lake. At one time, the area used to be made up of three parts – Lower Hambleton, Upper Hambleton and Middle Hambleton. In

The Finch's Arms is a stone-built country inn, renowned for the quality of its food. Meals can be eaten in the bar, or in the smart Garden Room restaurant to the rear of the building, from where there are magnificent views across Rutland Water. There is also an outdoor terrace and a beer garden. The choice of dishes changes regularly, and examples include roasted sea bream with spring vegetables and fennel leaves, honey-glazed duck breast with green pepper sauce, and lighter snacks such as goats cheese, plum tomato and basil panini. Grainstore ales are served, plus a weekly changing guest beer.

> **Distance:** 3¼ miles
>
> OS Explorer 234 Rutland Water
> GR 900076
>
> An easy walk, with a gradual incline at the end

Starting point: The car park at the Finch's Arms. Please obtain the landlord's permission to leave your car whilst walking.

How to get there: Turn off the A606 on a minor road about 1¼ miles east of Oakham, and continue for about 2 miles. The Finch's Arms is on your left, opposite the church.

Opening times are 11 am to 11 pm on Monday to Saturday, and 12 noon to 10.30 pm on Sunday. Food is served from 12 noon to 2.30 pm and 6.30 pm to 9.30 pm on Monday to Saturday, and from 12 noon to 9.30 pm on Sunday.

Telephone: 01572 756575.

The Walk

1 Leave the front entrance of the pub and turn left along the road. Ignore a road off to the right and keep straight ahead, passing a row of pretty cottages. Take the first signed path on the left, and go over an iron gate at the edge of a field. Aim diagonally right and drop downhill, passing a large tree on your right.

2 At the far side of the field go over another iron gate, and then turn right along a gravel track, which curves to the left slightly, before dropping downhill. The path, which is also used by cyclists,

then bends round to the right, from where there are good views across Rutland Water. Walk over a cattle grid, then continue through a wooded area. Follow the twists and turns of the clearly defined path, which eventually takes you up a gentle slope, before turning sharply to the right. Soon after, cross another cattle grid and continue to a junction of tracks.

3 Ignore a narrow road to your right, but go straight ahead. On reaching a track a few yards further on, turn right, and continue with the line of a hedge to your right. The track runs parallel with the road for about 220 yards, before taking

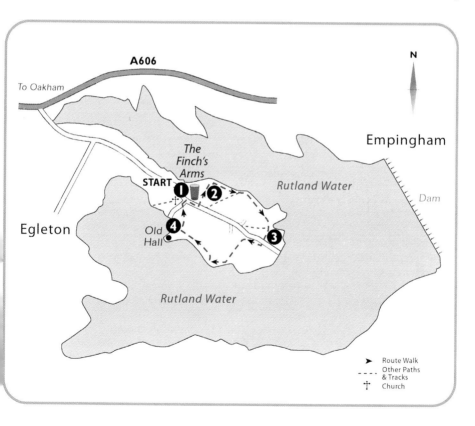

Rutland Water

you round a sharp left-hand bend, which leads downhill towards the water. At the bottom of the hill, turn right. Pass through a wooded area and follow the path round to the right, then the left. Further on, you pass through Hambleton Wood, which is managed by Leicestershire and Rutland Wildlife Trust. In spring, you may hear nightingales singing here. Once through the wood, there are good views across Rutland Water. Look out for ospreys, which can sometimes be seen fishing around here throughout spring and summer. Rutland Water is one of the few places in England where this rare bird of prey breeds. Further ahead, cross a cattle grid.

❹ Immediately afterwards, go over a stile on your right. Follow an unmarked path uphill. Towards the top of the hill, go over two stiles in quick succession, then cross a field (if cattle are present here, dogs should be kept under strict control). At the far side of the field, go over another stile, then walk ahead to a narrow road. Bear right here and walk uphill. Pass St Andrew's church on the left, then turn left at a T-junction. After a few yards, you will be back at the Finch's Arms.

Place of Interest

Anglian Water Birdwatching Centre is situated at Egleton, on the western edge of Rutland Water, and is close to Upper Hambleton. Ospreys can be seen from the bird hides and there is also an exhibition room and gift shop. Telephone: 01572 770651.

Date walk completed:

....

The Berkeley Arms

This enjoyable walk starts at Wymondham, the charming village that is believed to be the birthplace of the famous Stilton cheese. It also has an interesting old windmill, which can be seen for miles around. The route takes you along open fields bordered by streams and woodland, and although there are a few gentle slopes, much of the terrain is fairly flat. There are some excellent views to be enjoyed.

The Berkeley Arms dates back at least 250 years. This attractive pub has a main bar with a tiled floor and a separate non-smoking restaurant. There are also beamed ceilings and, in winter, real fires. Food is served throughout and examples include snacks like baguettes, light meals like goats cheese tartlet, and main dishes like venison, steaks and Thai curries. There is also a beer garden. Regular beers are Marston's Pedigree and Greene King IPA. A changing guest ale is also available.

Distance: *5½ miles*

OS Explorer 247 Grantham
GR 851188

An easy walk over mainly flat ground

Starting point: The Berkeley Arms car park. Please obtain the landlord's permission to leave your car whilst walking.

How to get there: Wymondham is situated 6 miles east of Melton Mowbray, off the B676. The pub can be found on Main Street.

Opening times are 6 pm to 11 pm on Monday to Wednesday, 12 noon to 2.30 pm and 6 pm to 11 pm on Thursday, 12 noon to 2.30 pm and 5.30 pm to 11 pm on Friday, 12 noon to 3 pm and 6 pm to 11 pm on Saturday, and 12 noon to 3 pm and 7 pm to 10.30 pm on Sunday. Food is served from 6.30 pm to 8.45 pm on Wednesday, 12 noon to 2 pm and 6.30 pm to 8.45 pm on Thursday and Friday, 12 noon to 2 pm and 7 pm to 9 pm on Saturday, and 12 noon to 2.30 pm on Sunday.

Telephone: 01572 787587.

The Walk

1 With the pub behind you, turn left along the pavement. Pass Butt Lane on your left and continue. Go over a stile on your left to follow a signed path. Immediately after passing houses to your left, bear slightly right across a grassy field. Pass under a line of telegraph poles and go through a kissing gate. The path curves to the right then the left, taking you across a dismantled railway line. Go through a metal gate and walk straight ahead across a field. Cross a footbridge over a ditch and then follow the marker arrow straight on. Cross another footbridge at the far side of the field and then bear slightly right. Pass a farm on your left and continue ahead, then bear slightly left at a marker post and go through a gap in the hedge to cross a footbridge. Continue ahead to a narrow lane.

2 Cross the lane and go through a gap in the hedge, then continue ahead. Cross a footbridge soon after and continue in the same direction. Cross another footbridge and follow the marker arrow straight on. Further on, follow a marker post straight ahead, keeping a hedge to your left. At the end of a field, cross a footbridge and turn left, then immediately right. Continue ahead, with a hedge to your left. Further on, the path becomes a stony track. Pass a wood on your left and then follow a marker arrow to the right. Turn left after about 60 yards and, at the bottom of an incline, turn left again. Turn right at a marker post soon after and cross a stream, before walking up a gentle incline. As the ground levels

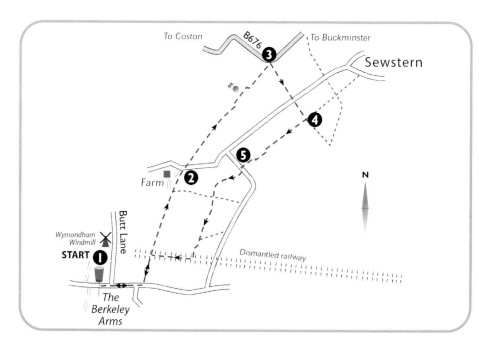

there are good views behind you and to your right.

③ As you reach a road further on (the B676), turn right along a signed byway. This takes you down a gentle incline and then up a slope. Keep going on the main track and cross a narrow lane further ahead. Continue on the byway for about 200 yards to arrive at a junction of marked tracks.

④ Turn right here and then walk straight ahead, keeping a narrow brook to your left. Go over a stile at the end of a field and cross a track, before continuing straight on, still with the brook to your left. Go over a stile at the far side of a field and turn left along a track. Turn right after a few yards and continue, now with the brook to your right. After 250 yards, go through a gap in the hedge on your right to cross the brook, then turn immediately left and continue with the brook to your left once more. At a marker arrow further on, go straight ahead across a field and continue to a narrow road.

⑤ Turn left along the road and, after crossing over the brook, go over a stile on your right and follow a signed path. Cross a grassy field and go over a stile, then bear round to the right slightly. Follow the path as it curves to the left then the right. Cross a footbridge over a brook on your right, then turn immediately left and continue with the brook to your left. Go over a stile and continue straight on. Soon after passing a stand of trees to your right, veer slightly right and go over a stile. Go

Nearing the end of the walk

through a metal gate and turn left, keeping a wire fence to your left. Follow the path round to the right, then turn left to go through the gate encountered near the start of the walk. Cross the dismantled railway line and retrace your steps across the grassy field. Turn right along the road and continue back to the pub.

Place of Interest

Wymondham Windmill is located on Butt Lane, 400 yards north of the pub. This partly restored tower mill was built circa 1814. Originally, it had six sails, and is one of a few such mills still remaining. There is also a tearoom, craft shops, an adventure playground and a small wood with native British trees. Telephone: 01572 787304.

Date walk completed:

....

The Peacock Inn

The small village of Croxton Kerrial marks the starting point for this satisfying walk. The route takes you over rolling farmland, peppered with copses and streams. From the higher ground, there are some marvellous views stretching out across the Vale of Belvoir, and along one section of the walk, the imposing Belvoir Castle can be glimpsed on the horizon. The return leg of the journey brings you back along a wide track and through the quiet village streets.

The Peacock Inn is around 300 years old, and is said to be haunted by a ghost called Mary. Very much a dining pub, the large main bar has stripped wooden floors and attractive décor. All food is home-made, and examples include traditional fish and chips, and fillet steak stuffed with Stilton cheese, wrapped in smoked bacon and served in a red wine and veal jus. John Smith's Bitter is available, alongside local guest ales. There is a large garden and courtyard, and even a hairdressing salon on site.

Opening times are 12 noon to 3 pm and 6.30 pm to 11 pm on Monday to Saturday, and 12 noon to 3 pm and 6.30 pm to 10.30 pm on Sunday. Food is served from 12 noon to 2.30 pm throughout the week, and in the evenings from 6.30 pm to 9.30 pm on Tuesday to Saturday, and 6.30 pm to 8.30 pm on Sunday and Monday.

Telephone: 01476 870324.

Distance: *4 miles*

OS Explorer 247 Grantham
GR 834291

An easy walk, with one short, steep climb

Starting point: The Peacock Inn's car park. Please obtain the landlord's permission to leave your car whilst walking.

How to get there: Croxton Kerrial is located 9 miles north-east of Melton Mowbray, off the A607. The Peacock Inn is situated where School Lane meets the A607.

The Walk

1 With the inn behind you, cross the A607 with caution and walk straight ahead along The Nook. Branch off to the right after a few yards to follow a signed path. Go through a gate further on and continue ahead. At the far side of a field, follow a marker arrow ahead, keeping a hedge to your left. Follow the path as it curves gently to the right, then continue ahead. Go through a gap in the hedge and carry on along the edge of a field until you reach a junction of tracks.

2 Turn right along the track and, where it bends to the right, go through a gate in front of you to follow a marked path ahead. Walk down a gentle incline, keeping a shallow stream down to your right. Near the bottom of a slope, turn right along a well-surfaced track and cross a cattle grid, then turn immediately left and cross a footbridge over a stream. Go through a gate and head slightly left to walk up Windmill Hill, where there are good views to your right and behind you. Go through a metal kissing gate at the top of the hill and continue straight ahead. Go over a stile and bear diagonally right across a field, to arrive at the A607.

3 Cross the road with care and follow the signed path on the opposite side, keeping a hedge to your right. Go through a kissing gate and bear slightly left, then continue ahead, keeping a wire fence to your left. As you drop downhill, you can see Belvoir Castle on the distant horizon. Go over two stiles at the bottom of the hill and walk ahead across a field. Cross another stile and head slightly right. Go

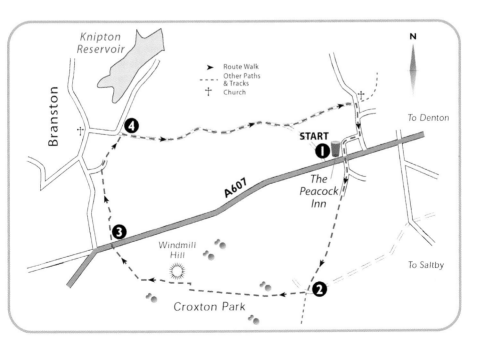

The view near the beginning of the walk

over a stile at the far side of the field to arrive at a junction of tracks. Turn right along the track and then follow it round to the left. Go through a gate and then turn diagonally right along a marked path. At the far side of a field, drop down a slope and cross a narrow stream, then continue ahead. Cross a stile to arrive at a track by a bend in the road.

4 Turn right along the track and then continue as it sweeps round to the left. Pass an old barn on your right and continue up a gentle incline. The ground levels for a while, before dropping downhill. Follow the path as it curves to the left then the right. Cross a stream further on and continue on the wide path. Further on, the muddy path becomes a well-surfaced track. Follow it round to the left and up a gentle incline. Pass houses and continue to a T-junction. Cross the road here and then turn right along the pavement. Pass the old police house on your left and then turn right along School Lane. Follow it round to the left to return to the Peacock Inn.

Date walk completed:

....

Places of Interest

Belvoir Castle is situated 3 miles north of Croxton Kerrial. This picturesque castle is the ancestral home of the Duke and Duchess of Rutland, and also houses the Queen's Royal Lancers Museum. Telephone: 01476 871000.

Woolsthorpe Manor (National Trust) is located 6¼ miles to the south-east of Croxton Kerrial. This 17th-century manor house was the birthplace and family home of Sir Isaac Newton. Telephone: 01476 860338.

The Peacock Inn

while others claim that in an ancient battle the road from the nearby castle ran red with blood. This short but enjoyable route takes you beside a stretch of the Grantham Canal, before looping back through farmland and, finally, past the village houses, many of which date back to the 1800s.

R edmile is an attractive rural village, situated in the Vale of Belvoir – pronounced 'Beever'. Rather appropriately, Belvoir means 'beautiful view' in French, and dates back to Norman times. There is some confusion as to how the village itself acquired its name. Some say it is because of the rich red earth found in the locality,

The welcoming **Peacock Inn** enjoys a quiet position on the banks of the canal. Inside you will find beamed ceilings and, in winter, roaring log fires. There is an extensive selection of good quality food, which is served either in the bars, outside, or in the restaurant areas. You can choose from delicious dishes such as smoked salmon crêpes with creamy chive sauce, beef in black pepper sauce, or snacks like pork and apple baguette. On Sundays there is always a choice of three different roasts. Timothy Taylor Landlord is available, alongside guest ales and a selection of wines by the glass.

Distance: 3 miles

*OS Explorer 260 Nottingham
GR 796355*

An easy walk on flat ground

Starting point: The Peacock Inn's car park. Please ask the landlord before leaving your car while you walk. Alternatively, use the road outside.

How to get there: From the A52 between Grantham and Nottingham, turn off to the south along Belvoir Road, 6½ miles west of Grantham, then turn right at a crossroads. The pub is on your right, next to the church.

Opening times are from 11 am to 11 pm on Monday to Saturday, and from 12 noon to 10.30 pm on Sunday. Lunch is served from 12 noon to 2 pm on Monday to Saturday, and from 12 noon to 3 pm on Sunday. Evening meals are available from 7 pm to 9 pm throughout the week.

Telephone: 01949 842554.

The Walk

❶ Leave the pub and turn right along the road. Cross the hump-backed bridge with care and, immediately afterwards, turn right to descend a series of steps, which brings you to a towpath beside the Grantham Canal. Turn left along the path and walk away from the bridge. The canal runs for 33 miles from the market town of Grantham to the River Trent at Nottingham. It was conceived and constructed in the 1790s, but was eventually closed to all traffic in 1929. However, it is now undergoing a restoration towards full navigation. The canal is under the care of British Waterways, and responsible walking is encouraged. Continue on the towpath for 1¼ miles, keeping a lookout for wildlife as you go.

❷ As you reach a bridge, walk up a slope to the left of it, to arrive at a road. Turn right and walk along the road with care. After a while, you pass Hill Farm on your left-hand side. Walk ahead, passing a road to the left and a signed byway to the right. After 300 yards, take the marked footpath on the right and follow it across a field. If you look to your left, you will see Belvoir Castle on the horizon. This fine building is the ancestral home of the Duke and Duchess of Rutland, and is the fourth castle to have stood on the site since Norman times. At the far side of the field,

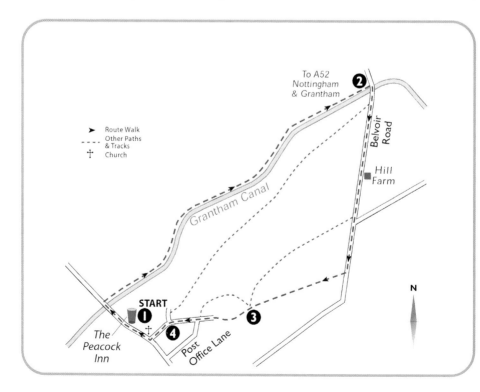

The church of St Peter, near the end of the walk

go through a gap in the hedge and continue diagonally right, until you reach a wide track.

3 Turn left and follow the path as it sweeps round to the right in a wide arc. Where the path ends, go straight ahead on a narrow road that runs between houses. Walk past Post Office Lane on your left and continue straight on.

4 Take the next road on the left (Baker's Lane) and walk to the end of it. Opposite you are some fine examples of old village houses. Turn right and pass the impressive St Peter's church, then walk straight ahead and back to the starting point at the pub.

Date walk completed:

....

Place of Interest

Belvoir Castle, which is also home to the Queen's Royal Lancers Museum, is situated about 1½ miles south-east of the village. Telephone: 01476 871000.

The Stilton Cheese Inn

in the film *A Bridge Too Far*. The plan was to capture five key bridges in Holland. A piece of the bridge at Arnhem was brought back to Somerby, and can be seen in the village hall to this day. This enjoyable route takes you over rolling hills and open fields, from where there are fabulous views for miles around.

The Stilton Cheese Inn is a lovely stone building, built circa 1700, with a patio area at the back. There are two bars and an upstairs restaurant, all of which have a cosy atmosphere. Food is served throughout, and examples from the menu include fish and chips, home-made lasagne and poached salmon steak with Hollandaise sauce. There is also a specials board. Regular beers are Marston's Pedigree, Tetley's Bitter and Grainstore Ten Fifty, alongside two changing guest ales.

Somerby is an unspoilt village set amid beautiful countryside. During the Second World War, paratroopers were billeted here before embarking on Operation Market Garden – immortalised

Distance: 4¼ miles

OS Explorers 246 Loughborough and 233 Leicester & Hinkley
GR 777105

A moderate walk over rolling ground

Starting point: The car park at the Stilton Cheese Inn, but please seek the landlord's permission to leave your car whilst walking.

How to get there: Somerby is situated 4 miles south of Melton Mowbray, off the A606. The pub can be found on High Street.

Opening times are 12 noon to 3 pm and 6 pm to 11 pm on Monday to Saturday, and 12 noon to 3 pm and 7 pm to 10.30 pm on Sunday. Food is available from 12 noon to 2 pm and 6 pm to 9 pm on Monday to Saturday, and from 12 noon to 2 pm and 7 pm to 9 pm on Sunday.

Telephone: 01664 454394.

The Walk

1 With the pub behind you, turn right along High Street, then turn right along Manor Lane. Go through a gate at the end of the lane and walk ahead on a signed bridleway. After another gate, bear slightly left down an incline. Keep a hedge to your left and go through a wooden gate. Carry on downhill, with a stream and a hedge over to your left. You come to a metal gate, after which you walk across a grassy field. Go through another gate soon after and follow the marker arrow ahead. Veer left after about 100 yards and cross a footbridge spanning a stream. Turn right and, at the corner of a field, bear round to the left. Go through a gap in the hedge to your right, then turn left and walk uphill. Further on, turn left at a marker arrow and then turn right by a wooden bench and walk downhill. Cross a footbridge and continue ahead. At the bottom of a slope, bear right to arrive at a narrow lane.

2 Turn left along the lane and then turn right at a T-junction. Pass a signed path on the right and walk along the road. Turn right along a signed bridleway and follow the wide track as it curves to the left. Pass a large house on your left and continue ahead, keeping a hedge to your right. Drop downhill and cross a footbridge over a stream, then continue ahead up an incline. Further on, you arrive at a junction of tracks.

3 Turn right and walk downhill, where there are great views ahead. Follow the path and cross stepping-stones in a stream, then continue ahead. Follow the path round to the left then the right, to arrive at a narrow lane. Turn left along the lane. Ignore a footpath to the right, but continue for 300 yards and turn right along a signed bridleway, keeping a hedge to your left. Further on, the path curves to the right slightly, now with a hedge to your right. At a junction of marked

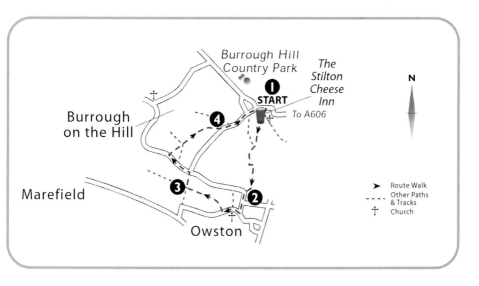

Looking back towards Somerby near the start of the walk

tracks, bear round to the left and then go through a gate on your right, to follow a marked bridleway heading north-east. Further on, walk between two gateposts and bear slightly left. Where the hedge to your left ends, follow a marker arrow straight ahead and across a field. Go through a wooden gate, where there are good views to the left, and turn diagonally right to walk up an incline. Go through another gate and continue ahead to reach a narrow lane.

4 Turn left along the lane. Ignore a marked path on the left and follow the road round to the right. Continue past stables on your right to reach a bend in the road in front of you. Turn right here and the pub is reached after 200 yards.

Place of Interest
Burrough Hill Country Park is located a mile to the north-west of Somerby, just off an unclassified road. The hill is one of the highest points in the county, and is crowned by an Iron Age hill fort with well-preserved ramparts. Information at the summit indicates the landmarks that can be seen. Open daily throughout the year. Telephone: 0116 2671944.

Date walk completed:

....

The Bewicke Arms

Open farmland, gentle hills, and attractive woods and streams are all waiting to be discovered on this exhilarating walk. The starting point is the picturesque village of Hallaton, noted for an ancient and eccentric tradition. Every Easter Monday, the village hosts its bottle-kicking contest and hare pie scramble. After the rector has distributed pieces of pie to a jostling crowd, teams from Hallaton and the neighbouring village of Medbourne engage in a free-for-all, as they try to capture three bottles for their respective villages. The bottles are actually small wooden casks, two of which are filled with ale, while the third is a dummy. The victors can then drink the contents.

The Bewicke Arms is a 400-year-old thatched inn with real fires in winter and a friendly atmosphere. Food is served in the two main bars and in the separate non-smoking eating area. Examples from the menu include chicken with Boursin cream sauce, beef and ale pie and home-made lasagne. Flowers IPA is always available, together with changing guest ales. There is a beer garden at the rear and an adjacent teashop (open daily from 10 am to 5 pm).

Opening times are 12 noon to 2.30 pm and 6 pm to 11 pm on Monday to Saturday, and 12 noon to 3 pm and 6 pm to 10.30 pm on Sunday. Food is available from 12 noon to 2 pm and 7 pm to 9.30 pm throughout the week.

Telephone: 01858 555217.

Distance: *6¼ miles*

OS Explorer 233 Leicester & Hinkley GR 788964

A moderate walk on undulating ground; muddy in places

Starting point: The car park at the Bewicke Arms. Please obtain the landlord's permission to leave your car whilst walking.

How to get there: Turn southwards on an unclassified road off the A47 east of Leicester, 5 miles from Uppingham. Drive straight ahead into Hallaton, and the pub can be found on Eastgate, not far from the church.

The Walk

1 Leave the pub car park and turn left along the road. Pass the medieval butter cross on your right, which was used by farmers' wives as a place to sell dairy produce, and then turn right along Churchgate. Walk past the church on your left, and follow the road round to the right. Beyond the school, veer round to the left.

2 Where the road runs out, walk straight ahead along a marked path. Go through a wooden gate and drop downhill. Cross a stile and, immediately afterwards, go over a footbridge. Turn left here and continue, before crossing a footbridge over a stream. Walk up a slope and cross another stile, then bear slightly right. The path takes you up a gentle incline. Further ahead, cross two stiles in quick succession

and then bear slightly right to go over a field. Pass a marker post at the far side of the field and keep straight ahead as you drop downhill. Near the bottom of the hill, bear slightly right and pass another marker post, then cross a footbridge over a stream. Keep straight ahead and, at the top of a slope, go through an iron gate to arrive at the edge of a farmyard.

3 Walk straight on, then follow the track as it curves to the left. An arrow on a wall then guides you right, to pass a barn on your left-hand side. Go through a wooden gate and then an iron gate, at which point turn right. After a few yards, turn slightly left to follow an unmarked, but well-defined path across a field. At the far corner of the field, bear right and continue, keeping a hedge to your left. Further on, go through a kissing gate on your left, then turn immediately right.

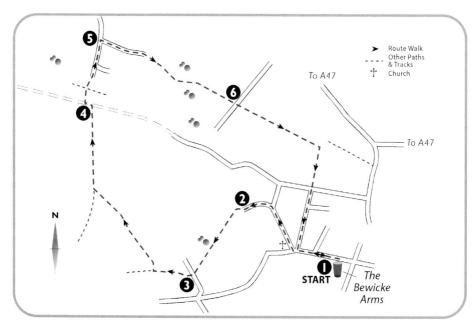

After about 60 yards, go diagonally left along a poorly-defined track. Soon after, turn right along an indistinct path and then go over a wooden fence. Continue to a well-surfaced track.

4 Turn left here and, after 40 yards, turn right along a signed path. Keep straight ahead, ignoring a marked path off to the right. Further on, a marker post guides you straight on. Continue with a hedge to your left. Eventually, the grassy track becomes a well-surfaced farm track. Go straight ahead, passing buildings to your left and then follow the track downhill.

5 At a marker post, turn right along a well-surfaced track through a farm complex. Where the track bends right, go straight ahead over a field and continue until you reach a gravel track. Turn left along the track, which then bends to the right. Cross a bridge over a stream, then follow the track round to the left. Take the next signed path on the right and aim for a marker post by a wood. Go through a kissing gate and keep straight ahead, with the wood to your left. The path takes you up a gentle incline before curving to the left. Go through a kissing gate and cross a field, then go through another kissing gate and keep straight ahead until you reach a gravel track.

6 Cross the track and go through a kissing gate. At the end of a field, walk straight ahead along an unmarked, but well-trodden path. Go through a kissing gate at a junction of paths and then turn right, keeping a hedge to your right. At

The medieval butter cross at Hallaton

the end of the field, go through a kissing a gate and continue to the road junction. Go straight ahead along Hunt's Lane. Pass Hog Lane on your left, then keep going downhill. Turn left along Churchgate, then left again, to retrace your steps back to the pub.

Place of Interest

Hallaton Village Museum is situated on Hog Lane, and houses fascinating exhibits relating to the bottle-kicking contest and hare pie scramble, as well as heritage information. It is open from 2.30 pm to 5 pm on weekends and bank holidays between May and October. Telephone: 01858 555388.

Date walk completed:

....

The Black Horse

Grimston is a charming rural village centred around a pretty green. A large stone boulder stands on the green and legend has it that it was thrown there by an angry giant called Grim – hence the name Grimston. This attractive route takes you through gently rolling farmland, alongside woods and streams.

Distance: *5 miles*

OS Explorer 246 Loughborough
GR 684219

A moderate walk over undulating ground

Starting point: Outside the Black Horse.

How to get there: Grimston lies between the A46 and the A606. Taking the A6006, turn off northwards along an unclassified road, 3 miles west of Melton Mowbray. Turn left after ½ mile and continue straight ahead into Grimston. The pub is on Main Street, overlooking the village green. It does not have a car park, but you can park on the roadside close by.

You also pass through the village of Saxelbye, which is one of the few places where Stilton cheese is made.

The Black Horse is an attractive, welcoming pub. Inside there is a lounge bar with beamed ceilings, and a separate restaurant area. A wide choice of food is available, including lighter meals like omelettes and ploughman's lunches, through to main dishes such as chicken breast with Stilton and walnut sauce. Marston's Pedigree and Greene King Abbot Ale are regulars at the pumps, and at least one guest beer is always available. You will find a beer garden and a petanque piste at the rear of the building.

Opening times are 12 noon to 3 pm and 6 pm to 11 pm on Monday to Saturday, and 12 noon to 10.30 pm on Sunday. Food is available from 12 noon to 2 pm and 6 pm to 9 pm on Monday to Saturday, and from 12 noon to 4 pm and 6 pm to 9 pm on Sunday.

Telephone: 01664 812358.

The Walk

1 With the pub behind you, turn left along the main road. Pass the church and follow the road round to the right. Go through a gate and follow a signed bridleway on your left. Walk through a small farmyard immediately afterwards to reach a gate and cross a grassy field. Go through an iron gate at the end of the field and turn left, then immediately right. Follow the bridleway down a gentle incline, keeping a hedge to your right. At the bottom of the slope, pass through a gate and cross a footbridge over a narrow drainage ditch (dismantled railway), then bear diagonally right. Go through a wooden gate, walking past a farmhouse on your left. Continue up a gentle incline and, where the track bends to the left, go straight ahead. At the bottom of a slope, pass a marker post and bear slightly left. Walk up an incline to a narrow lane.

2 Turn left along the lane and take the next marked bridleway on the right. Follow it round to the left and down a slope, then walk up a gentle incline and pass a wood on your right. Keep to the main track, as you pass underneath power lines. The path then curves to the right and left, before taking you past attractive houses. Continue ahead on a well-surfaced lane and walk down a gentle incline to reach a staggered crossroads.

3 Go straight ahead and then turn right by a notice board to follow a bridleway straight ahead. Go through a gate and walk on. Veer slightly right soon after and go through a wooden gate, to walk into a short stretch of woodland. At the far edge of the wood follow a marker arrow, which guides you slightly right. Go through a gate and continue ahead, passing a wooded area to your right. Further on, pass a small lake to your right, then bear slightly right and walk down a gentle slope to reach another gate. Beyond this, follow the marker arrow

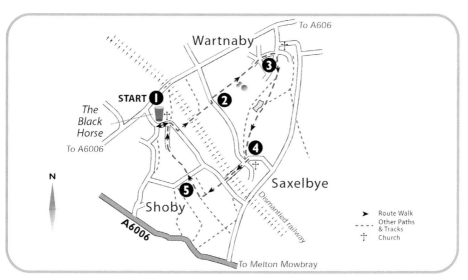

105

This boulder on the village green is said to have been thrown by a giant called Grim

crossroads and walk through the village of Saxelbye. Pass under a railway bridge and walk on to a T-junction. Turn right and, after a few yards, turn left and cross the road to follow a signed path straight ahead. After crossing a stream, bear slightly right and go over a stile located behind a large tree. Continue ahead, keeping a hedge to your right. Follow the path as it curves to the left and continue to a marker post near a tree. Turn right here and cross a field. Go over a stile and continue to a narrow lane.

5 Cross the lane and go through a kissing gate, then walk ahead. Go over a stile and bear slightly left to cross a field. Bear a little to the right at the edge of the field and continue with a hedge to your left. Further on, go over a stile on your left and bear slightly right. After 50 yards, go over a stile on your right and head to the left across a grassy field. Go over two stiles in quick succession and walk on. Bear slightly left further on and go over a stile, then continue ahead. Go over two more stiles and then bear round to the right along a wide track. As you pass houses, the track becomes a lane. Turn left at a T-junction to return to the pub.

straight ahead. Continue with a brook over to your right and go through a gate at the end of a field. Walk ahead and pass under power lines, then follow the path as it curves slightly left, bringing you to a lane.

4 Turn right along the lane, then follow it round to the left. Go straight ahead at a

Date walk completed:

....

Place of Interest

Melton Carnegie Museum is located on Thorpe End in Melton Mowbray, 5 miles to the south-east of Grimston. The museum shows the life and times of this thriving market town – internationally renowned as the birthplace of the humble pork pie – through displays and exhibitions. Open all year round. Telephone: 01664 569946.

Saddington 34
The Queen's Head

Part of the route takes you beside a stretch of the Grand Union Canal, where you can see colourful narrowboats. If you're lucky, you may also glimpse a kingfisher darting by, or a fox dashing between the hedgerows and trees. On the return leg of the journey, there are fine views from the higher ground, towards Saddington Reservoir and beyond.

Saddington is a quiet village set in a scenic location. This satisfying walk leads you over clear streams, past beautiful woodland and over rolling hills.

Distance: **5 miles**

OS Explorer 223 Northampton & Market Harborough
GR 658918

A moderate walk, with some short, steep climbs

Starting point: The car park at the Queen's Head. Please seek the landlord's permission to leave your car whilst walking.

How to get there: From the A6 south-east of Leicester, turn off southwards and drive through Kibworth Beauchamp. After passing through Smeeton Westerby, head west on an unclassified road to Saddington. The Queen's Head is situated close to the church.

The Queen's Head dates back to at least 1747. Inside there is a main bar, which merges with a smoking and non-smoking restaurant area. There are snacks such as baguettes and home-made lasagne, through to main meals like pine nut crusted sea bass served on sautéed garlic potatoes. Everards Beacon Bitter and Tiger are always available, together with two changing guest ales. Outside, a beautiful beer garden overlooks the nearby reservoir.

Opening times are 12 noon to 3 pm and 7 pm to 11 pm on Monday, 12 noon to 3 pm and 5.30 pm to 11 pm on Tuesday to Friday, 12 noon to 3 pm and 6 pm to 11 pm on Saturday, and 12 noon to 6 pm on Sunday. Food is served at lunchtime from 12 noon to 2 pm on Monday to Saturday, and from 12.30 pm to 4 pm on Sunday. Evening meals are available from 6.30 pm to 9 pm on Tuesday to Saturday.

Telephone: 0116 2402536.

The Walk

1 Leave the pub car park and turn right, then turn right along the next road. Take the first signed path on your right. Go over a stile and continue straight ahead. Go over two stiles in quick succession and continue across a grassy field. Follow the path downhill and then cross a stream. Walk straight ahead and cross two footbridges over two separate streams. Immediately after crossing the second, turn left to follow a well-trodden path. Go over a stile and follow the path as it curves gently to the left. Further on, go over an iron gate and bear diagonally right. Walk up an incline and cross a footbridge over a narrow stream, then turn half-left and walk up a gentle slope. The ground levels out before dropping downhill slightly. Keep a line of hawthorn trees to your left, then go through an iron gate on your left to cross a footbridge over the Grand Union Canal.

2 On the far side of the bridge, go through a wooden gate on your right and walk along a signed path, keeping a hedge to your right. After about 100 yards, veer slightly left and follow the path down a gradual slope. Cross a stile by a marker post and then go straight ahead. Cross another stile and continue straight on until you reach a road. Turn right along the road and, after about 450 yards, turn right along a farm track.

3 As you reach a bridge spanning the canal, leave the track by the right and turn left, to pass underneath the bridge. Continue along the towpath, with the canal to your right. In spring and summer this is a good place to see water birds. Keep to the towpath and pass under a bridge further ahead. Keep going and, immediately after passing under the next bridge, turn left and go over a stile. Turn left, then left again, before crossing the bridge to the other side of the canal. Follow a marker post, which guides you straight ahead and up a gradual slope. As you reach a house on your left, veer slightly right, aiming for a marker post. From here, go straight ahead until you reach a road.

4 Turn right and walk along the road with care. At a junction further on, go

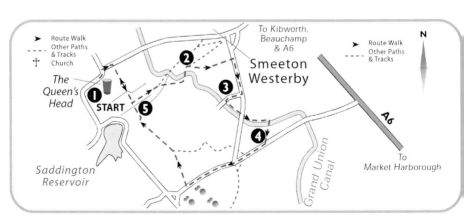

108

Crossing the bridge over the Grand Union Canal

straight ahead and climb uphill. After passing a wood on your left, take the next signed path on your right. Keep the line of a hedge to your right and walk downhill. Go over two stiles in quick succession and continue straight on. At the bottom of the hill, go over two stiles and continue. At the far side of a field, cross a stile and bear half-left, to follow a clearly defined path uphill. Pass a copse on your left and then look back for some great views. At the top of the hill go straight ahead, passing bushes to your left and keeping the line of a hedge close to your right. Go over a stile and then continue on a well-defined track. At the far side of a field, go over a stile and continue with a hedge to your left. From here, there are good views over Saddington Reservoir to your left. At the corner of a field, turn right and then climb over a stile on your left. Walk straight ahead and continue downhill. At the bottom of the hill, you meet a footbridge.

5 Cross the bridge and continue ahead.

A little further on, cross two more bridges (these were used near the start of the route) and keep going straight on. Go over two stiles and bear slightly left, as you walk uphill. Cross two stiles by a tree and walk ahead, retracing your steps from earlier. Go over another stile and walk uphill to a road. Turn left then left again, retracing your steps back to the Queen's Head.

Place of Interest

Foxton Canal Museum, situated 2½ miles south-east of Saddington, is an award-winning museum that explains the heritage of the local canals. It stands next to a flight of 10 locks and is open all year round. Telephone: 0116 2792657.

Date walk completed:

....

The Royal Oak

walk along the canal towpath, passing locks and ponds along the way. Later, you continue beside the River Soar and pass through a scenic nature reserve, where a variety of interesting wildlife may be seen.

The Royal Oak is a traditional village pub dating back to the 19th century. There is a friendly atmosphere in the large bar, which has a designated non-smoking area. You will find a beer garden outside and Northamptonshire skittles can be played. Snacks include sandwiches and jacket potatoes, and main dishes could be fillet steak, mushroom stroganoff, or breast of chicken in Stilton sauce. Everards Beacon Bitter and Tiger are regulars at the pumps, and are accompanied by two changing guest ales.

Opening times are 5 pm to 11 pm on Monday, 12 noon to 3 pm and 5 pm to 11 pm on Tuesday to Friday, 12 noon to 11 pm on Saturday, and 12 noon to 10.30 pm on Sunday. Food is available from 12 noon to 2 pm on Tuesday, 12 noon to 2 pm and 7 pm to 9 pm on Wednesday to Saturday, and 12 noon to 2.30 pm on Sunday (no food all day Monday or on Tuesday evening).

Telephone: 01509 813937.

This circuit starts in the quiet and ancient village of Cossington. The route takes you along open fields to a confluence of the River Wreake and the Grand Union Canal. From there, you

Distance: *3½ miles*

OS Explorer 246 Loughborough GR 606134

An easy walk on flat ground; muddy in places

Starting point: The Royal Oak's car park. Please seek the landlord's permission to leave your car whilst walking.

How to get there: Cossington is situated 5 miles to the south-east of Loughborough, between the A6 and the A46. The pub can be found on Main Street.

The Walk

1 Leave the main entrance of the pub and turn left along the pavement. Pass Back Lane on your left and continue to a T-junction. Cross the road with caution and walk straight ahead along a signed footpath. Soon after passing an old farm building on your left, you reach a pond in front of you. Follow the marker arrow round to the left, then bear slightly right to aim for a marker post at the edge of a field.

2 Go over a stile by the marker post, but do not cross the bridge in front of you. To your left you can see where the River Wreake joins the Grand Union Canal. Turn right and walk along the towpath, keeping the canal to your left. As you pass Junction Lock further on, there are good views to the left. Follow the towpath as it

curves round to the right. At a marker post, continue along the path as it bends to the left, taking you past fishing pools on your right-hand side. Go over a stile and continue. Further on, the River Soar joins the canal from the left. Cross a bridge here and walk straight ahead. Pass Cossington Lock on your left, then veer right to arrive at a road bridge.

3 Cross the road carefully and then turn right. At the far side of the bridge, descend wooden steps on your left and go over a stile, before continuing straight ahead. The fields to your right form part of Cossington Meadows Nature Reserve, which is owned and managed by Leicestershire and Rutland Wildlife Trust. Follow the well-trodden path as it curves to the right, keeping the River Soar to your left. Go through a kissing gate and walk on, then cross a stile and a

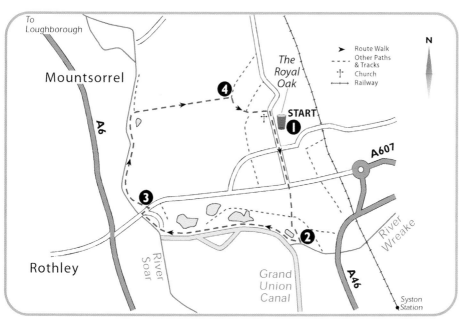

Looking back along the Grand Union Canal

footbridge further ahead. Pass through a small wood and then follow the path round to the left and right. Walk along the edge of a pool and turn right at a marker post, still with the pool to your right. Continue ahead, ignoring unmarked tracks to the left and right. Further on, you reach a marked junction of paths.

4 Turn right here, keeping trees to your left. Follow the marker arrows and continue, as the path bends to the left. Keep a narrow stream to your left and walk on. Further on, the path curves to the left, taking you across the stream. Go over a stile and walk straight ahead. Pass the church on your right to arrive at a road. Cross the road and turn right along the pavement and, after passing pretty

houses and cottages, you return to the pub.

Place of Interest

Bradgate Country Park is situated 5 miles to the south-west of Cossington. This medieval deer park includes the ruins of Bradgate House – birthplace of Lady Jane Grey, the nine-day Queen of England. There are woods, lakes and heathland to explore, and there is also a visitor centre and refreshments. Open all year. Telephone: 0116 2362713.

Date walk completed:

....

The Chequers

Located at the southern tip of the county, Swinford is an attractive and tranquil village with an impressive church and some pretty thatched cottages. The route winds its way through undulating farmland, woods and streams, and affords some fine views of the surrounding landscape. This is an under-walked area, so you should be able to enjoy the paths in peace.

Distance: 5½ miles

OS Explorer 222 Rugby & Daventry
GR 569794

A moderate walk, with some gentle slopes; muddy in places

Starting point: The car park at the Chequers. Please seek the landlord's permission to leave your car whilst walking.

How to get there: Swinford is situated off junction 19 of the M1 motorway. The pub is on High Street, opposite the church.

The Chequers is a friendly pub dating back to the 19th century. There is a large single bar, which includes a non-smoking area. Traditional pub games are played, among them table skittles, dominoes and cards. A selection from the menu could include chicken Kiev, buttered salmon steak or roast vegetable quiche. Adnams Bitter is served and a mild is usually available, together with other guest beers. Outside there is a large beer garden with children's play equipment.

Opening times are 7 pm to 11 pm on Monday (open at lunchtime and serving food on Bank Holiday Mondays), 12 noon to 2.30 pm and 6 pm to 11 pm on Tuesday to Saturday, and 12 noon to 3 pm and 7 pm to 10.30 pm on Sunday. Food is available from 12 noon to 2 pm and 6 pm to 9 pm Tuesday to Saturday, and 12 noon to 2 pm on Sunday.

Telephone: 01788 860318.

113

The Walk

1 Leave the main entrance of the pub and turn right along the road. Turn left along the next road and, as the main road bends to the right, turn left along Shawell Road. Go over a stile next to a marked path on your right, then bear half-left. Walk down a gentle slope and then cross a stile and footbridge, to arrive at the edge of a field. Bear half-right across the field, aiming for a marker post at the top of an incline. As you reach the post, turn left and continue ahead, keeping a hedge to your right. Further on, the path curves to the right slightly. Go over two stiles in quick succession, then bear left, keeping a hedge to your left. After about 450 yards, ascend a series of steps on your left, to arrive at a well-surfaced track.

2 Turn left and cross a bridge over the M1 motorway, then follow the track round to the left. The track then becomes a muddy bridleway. At a junction of tracks, go over two stiles on your right, then cross a grassy field and go over another stile. Bear slightly left before crossing two more stiles in quick succession. Go straight ahead and walk across a grassy field. Go over a stile at the far side of the field, then bear slightly left, passing a large oak tree on your left-hand side. Walk down a gentle slope and cross two stiles on your left, to arrive at a road.

3 Turn right along the road and walk down a gentle slope. After crossing a road bridge over a stream, continue straight ahead. Walk along the road up an incline and then turn right at a signed footpath (this is a new footpath route due to be operational at the time of publication; follow diversion notices if the work is not

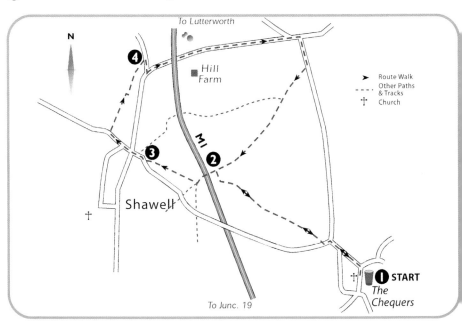

The scenery around point 3 of the walk

yet completed). Walk straight ahead along a raised bank and, further ahead, go through a kissing gate on your right, then turn immediately left and go through another kissing gate. Cross a track and go through a kissing gate, then bear slightly right to follow the path down a gentle incline. Further ahead pass a hut on your right and continue, before going over a stile to arrive at a narrow lane.

4 Turn right along the lane and, at a T-junction, turn left along the road. Continue as the road bends to the right, taking you underneath a bridge. Pass Hill Farm on your right and continue. Turn right at a T-junction, then bear right again along a road. After 110 yards, take the signed bridleway on your right. Go through a kissing gate, then go straight ahead, keeping a hedge to your right. Further on, ignore a path to your right, but follow the marker posts as they guide you straight on. Go through several gates until you reach a well-surfaced track. Follow it round until you can see the bridge over the M1, which you crossed

earlier on the route. Do not cross the bridge this time, but go over the stiles on your left, then turn right. Continue with a hedge to your right, retracing your steps from earlier. Further on, go over stiles on your right, then bear left. Cross the footbridge and stile encountered earlier on the walk, then walk up the slope and go over a stile beside a road. Turn left along the road, then right at the next road. Retrace your steps back to the pub.

Place of Interest

Stanford Hall, situated a mile to the east of Swinford, was built in the 1690s and is one of the finest examples of the architecture of that period. It houses fine portraits and furniture, and there is a caravan site located in the estate grounds. Telephone: 01788 860250.

Date walk completed:

....

The Dog and Hedgehog

The name Dadlington derives from Daedel – an Anglo-Saxon chieftain who established a settlement in the same area as the present village. After walking beside a scenic stretch of the Ashby-de-la-Zouch Canal, more history unfolds as you pass Bosworth battlefield and Ambion Hill. According to a widely believed 18th-century theory, it was here, in August 1485, that the armies of King Richard III and Henry Tudor faced each other, in what was to be Richard's last stand in the Wars of the Roses. The latest theory, however, places the battlefield about a mile further south, closer to Dadlington itself. And in January 2005, almost £1 million in National Lottery funding was made available to investigate further. The route then takes you through attractive woodland, and back along the canal to the starting point.

The Dog and Hedgehog dates back to the 18th century, although it is thought that there may have been a pub on the site since the 12th century. A framed print inside tells how the establishment got its unusual name. There is a large main bar and a separate restaurant upstairs. Food is served throughout and examples from the menu include fish and chips, shank of lamb and duck breast in green peppercorn sauce. Regular beers are Bass Bitter, Hook Norton Best Bitter and Church End Whittle Ale. Two changing guest beers are also available. Good views can be enjoyed from the beer garden at the rear.

Opening times are 12 noon to 2.30 pm and 5.30 pm to 11 pm on Monday to Saturday, and 12 noon to 10.30 pm on Sunday. Food is served from 12 noon to 2.30 pm and 6 pm to 9.30 pm on Monday to Saturday, and 12 noon to 9 pm on Sunday.

Telephone: 01455 212629.

Distance: *5½ miles*

OS Explorer 232 Nuneaton & Tamworth GR 403980

An easy walk, with a few short climbs

Starting point: The car park at the Dog and Hedgehog. Please obtain permission to leave your car whilst walking.

How to get there: Turn westwards off the A447 at Stapleton north of Hinckley, along an unclassified road, and drive into Dadlington. Turn right at a crossroads and continue: you will see the pub on your left.

The Walk

1 Leave the pub and turn left. Cross the road and go over a stile to follow a signed path heading slightly left. Bear right at a marker post, then cross a stile and turn right, keeping a wire fence to your right. Go over a stile further on and continue ahead, with a hedge to your right. Immediately after crossing a bridge over the Ashby-de-la-Zouch Canal, turn left to arrive at the towpath. Turn left and pass under the bridge, keeping the canal to your right. Pass under a road bridge further on and follow the towpath round to the left. Continue along the towpath and pass under another bridge. Follow the course of the canal round to the left and pass under bridge number 34 at Sutton Cheney Wharf. Keep to the towpath and, after passing Ambion Wood on the opposite bank, you reach a bridge.

2 Walk under the bridge and continue along the towpath as it curves to the right. At the next bridge, turn left and leave the towpath, then turn right along the road and cross the bridge over the canal. Carry on to Shenton railway station and turn right to follow a sign marked 'Battlefield Visitor Centre'. Alternatively, you may wish to walk ahead for 200 yards, to see the stone monument that marks the spot where King Richard III is said to have been slain. Cross the railway line with care and bear slightly left to follow a marked path that curves round to the right. This takes you to the top of Ambion Hill, where Richard III and the royal army are thought to have been camped before the fateful battle. Go through a gate at the top of the hill and turn left. Bear right after a few yards and then curve to the left to reach a well-surfaced track.

3 Turn right and pass the Bosworth Battlefield Visitor Centre on your left (drop in if you have time) and continue

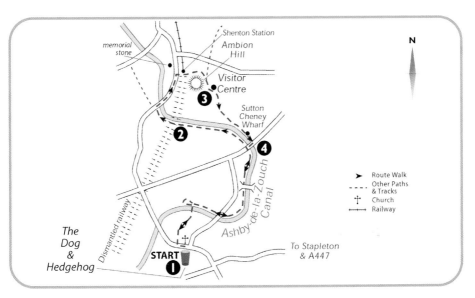

The Ashby-de-la-Zouch Canal

through gates. Follow the arrows into Ambion Wood. The track takes you round to the right then the left. Follow the path as it curves gently to the left, before bringing you to a path beside the canal. Continue with the canal to your right and pass a café at Sutton Cheney Wharf, where narrowboat trips can be booked. Soon after, veer slightly left and go over a stile to reach a road.

❹ Turn right and cross the bridge, then turn right to descend some wooden steps. Turn right to pass under the bridge (no 34) again and continue on the towpath, this time with the canal to your left. Retrace your steps along the towpath and, immediately after passing under the third bridge (no 31), turn right and then right again to cross the bridge once more. Walk

ahead along the edge of a field and cross a stile. Go over another stile on your left and walk the short distance back to the pub.

Place of Interest
Bosworth Battlefield Visitor Centre is passed on the route. It provides information on the battle as well as housing interesting exhibitions. Books can be purchased and there are also tours of the battlefield, special events and battle re-enactments. Refreshments are also available. Open from March to December. Telephone: 01455 290429.

Date walk completed:

....

The Falcon Inn

Long Whatton is a beautiful village, tucked away in the north-west corner of the county. It has some impressive buildings, including a fine church, timbered houses and some very attractive thatched cottages. Winding paths and tracks make their way through the surrounding countryside, which is a patchwork of rolling farmland, woods, meadows and clear brooks. A wide range of wildlife can be seen on this route throughout the year, but particularly during the spring and summer months.

Distance: 7½ miles

OS Explorer 245 The National Forest, Burton upon Trent & Swadlincote GR 478235

A moderate walk, with some slopes; can be muddy in places

Starting point: The Falcon Inn's car park. Please obtain the landlord's permission to leave your car whilst walking.

How to get there: Long Whatton is located between Loughborough and junction 23a of the M1. From Loughborough, head north-west on the A6 for 3 miles, then turn left along the B5324. Soon after, turn right into the village, where the pub can be found on Main Street, not far from the public telephone box.

The Falcon Inn has an attractive whitewashed exterior, complemented by pretty floral hanging baskets. Inside, the bar has a beamed ceiling, decorated with traditional tankards. Delicious dishes such as home-made steak and ale pie, and smoked haddock and spring onion fishcakes are served in a friendly atmosphere. Everards Tiger and Beacon bitters are on offer, alongside the occasional guest beer.

Opening times are 12 noon to 11 pm on Monday to Saturday, and 12 noon to 10.30 pm on Sunday. Food is served from 12 noon to 2 pm and 6.30 pm to 9.30 pm on Monday to Saturday, and 12 noon to 4 pm on Sunday.

Telephone: 01509 842416.

The Walk

1 Leave the pub and turn right along the road. After 450 yards, you pass the village church on your left. Soon after, go through an iron gate on your right, next to a footpath sign. Follow the path between the lines of two wooden fences; it then bends sharply to the right. The path twists and turns, before bringing you to a kissing gate. Go through the gate and bear half-left. As you walk up a gentle incline, you will see a yellow marker post beside a double stile, in the hedgerow ahead of you. Cross the stile and bear slightly left. Further on, a marker post directs you straight on, along the edge of a field. At the far side of the field, go over a stile and continue straight ahead. A little way on, go over another stile and keep straight ahead, with the line of a hedge to your left. Cross a stile next to a large tree, then aim diagonally right and continue to a marker post near the road.

2 Cross the road and go over a stile on the opposite side, to pick up the footpath once more. Continue straight on, passing a farm building on your right and a communications mast on your left. The path then bends to the right, before taking you over a bridge spanning the M1 motorway. Keep straight ahead, and peace is again resumed, as you turn left to skirt the edge of a wood. As the path curves to the right, there are good views ahead of you. After walking down a slope, you arrive at a farm track.

3 Turn right and walk along the track. Further on, ignore a footpath off to the right, but keep straight ahead. Immediately after passing a farm building on your left, go over a stile and continue,

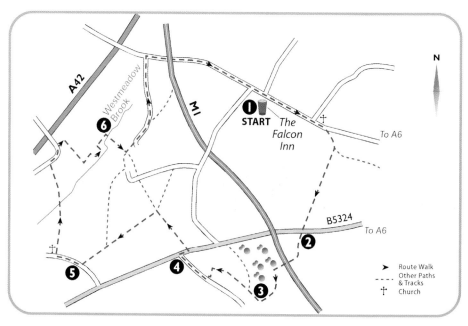

A fine view over the farmland near point 5 of the walk

keeping a hedge to your left. Go through a gate and across a field, then over a stile and across another field, before going through a gate. Once past the gate, bear right to arrive in a farmyard. Turn left and walk for 60 yards, where a marker post guides you left again, and on to a road. Turn right along the road and walk with care to a T-junction.

4 Turn right at the junction and, after 100 yards, cross the road to pick up a signed footpath. Keep straight ahead, with a fence to your left. At the far side of a field go through a kissing gate, then aim for the far left-hand corner of a field, passing a small stand of trees to your right

as you go. Cross a stile in the corner of the field, and walk straight ahead. Keep the line of a hedge to your left and continue to the far side of the field, where you reach a footpath sign. Ignore the two marked paths ahead and to your right, but instead turn sharp left to walk across a field (this path is not marked on the sign), heading roughly south-west. Go over a stile at the edge of a field and continue straight on. Go through a wooden gate then keep straight ahead, passing a stand of trees immediately to your left. A marker post guides you straight on. The path then curves to the left slightly, bringing you to another marker post. Go straight ahead here, keeping the line of a hedge to your left. The narrow path widens as you continue. Further on, ignore a path off to the right and continue to a road.

5 Turn right along the road and, after 100 yards, take the signed path on your right. Go through an iron gate, and at the edge of a field go straight ahead. Cross a stile, then bear half-left, heading downhill. As you walk, there are good views ahead and to your right. At the foot of the hill, cross a bridge over a brook then turn immediately right to go over a stile. Cross a field before going over another stile. Keep straight ahead and, as you reach a yellow marker post ahead of you, turn left, keeping a hedge to your right. As the hedge ends, go over a stile to arrive at a narrow road. Turn right along the road. Just before reaching a bridge over the A42, turn right along an unmarked track, which takes you down a gentle slope, running parallel with the main road. At the end of the track, go over a stile and then turn right, keeping a hedge to your right. Shortly before reaching the corner of a field, turn left and aim for a yellow marker post ahead of you. Cross a bridge over a brook, then go over a stile and continue, following the line of the brook. Cross a stile at the end of a field to reach a footbridge.

6 Turn right to cross the bridge over the brook. Continue to a junction of unmarked paths, then turn left, aiming for a marker post. Pass a wood on your right, and keep straight ahead when you reach a narrow lane. After about 850 yards, turn right at a T-junction and walk along the road with care. Pass under a road bridge and walk straight ahead along the pavement. After passing attractive houses, you arrive back at the Falcon Inn, on your right.

Date walk completed:

....

Place of Interest

Donington Park, situated 4½ miles north-west of the village, is an international Grand Prix class motor racing venue, which also houses the largest collection of Grand Prix cars in the world. Telephone: 01332 810048.

The Rising Sun

This walk can be enjoyed all year round, but during spring and summer it is particularly beautiful. Soon after leaving behind the tiny village of Shackerstone, you pass through peaceful wooded countryside. After a short stretch along country lanes, the return leg of the journey then takes you beside the bank of the Ashby-de-la-Zouch Canal, where there is an abundance of wildlife and picturesque scenery to be experienced along the way.

The Rising Sun is a delightful pub, which is around 300 years old. Inside there is a main bar with a stone floor and wood panelled walls. There is also a poolroom, a separate restaurant and a beer garden at the side of the building. A wide choice of food is available, and examples include home-made steak and ale pie, bacon and spinach crêpes and mushroom stroganoff. Regular ales are Timothy Taylor Landlord and Marston's Pedigree. Guest beers are also available.

Opening times are 12 noon to 2.30 pm and 6 pm to 11 pm on Monday to Friday, 11.30 am to 11 pm on Saturday, and 12 noon to 10.30 pm on Sunday. Food is served from 12 noon to 2 pm and 7 pm to 10 pm on Monday to Saturday, and 12 noon to 2.30 pm and 7 pm to 10 pm on Sunday.

Telephone: 01827 880215.

Distance: *4½ miles*

OS Explorer 232 Nuneaton & Tamworth GR 375067

An easy walk on flat ground

Starting point: The Rising Sun's car park, but please obtain the landlord's permission to leave your car while you walk.

How to get there: Shackerstone is situated 9 miles north of Nuneaton, off the A444. The Rising Sun can be found on Church Road.

The Walk

1 Leave the pub and turn right along Church Road, then turn right at a T-junction. Cross a road bridge over the canal and then turn right along a signed path. Follow the track round to the right. As you reach the train station, go through a gate on your left and cross a bridge over the railway line. Cross a stile and go diagonally right to follow a marked path. At the corner of a wood, go over a stile and then cross another stile on your right. From here, head diagonally left across a field and then cross a stile next to a house, which brings you to a narrow road.

2 Cross the road and follow a signed path heading diagonally left. Go over a stile next to a large dead tree and turn half-right. Walk across a field and cross a stile, then bear slightly left, aiming for a gap in the hedge ahead of you. Once there, go straight ahead on a clearly-defined track. Go over a stile and aim for the top left-hand corner of a field. Climb over a stile and walk straight ahead. Soon after, cross a footbridge and a stile, then walk up a gentle incline, keeping a hedge to your right. At a junction of paths at the top of the slope, turn right and then go over a stile on your left. Pass an impressive house on your left and then go through an iron gate. Bear slightly left and pass a private tennis court, before crossing a stile by the side of a road.

3 Turn right along the road and pass underneath a railway bridge. Soon after, ignore a road branching off to the right, but keep straight ahead. Cross a bridge over a stream and then follow the road round to the left. Cross a bridge over the Ashby-de-la-Zouch Canal and admire the views to the left and right.

4 At the far side of the bridge, turn right and walk along the towpath, keeping the

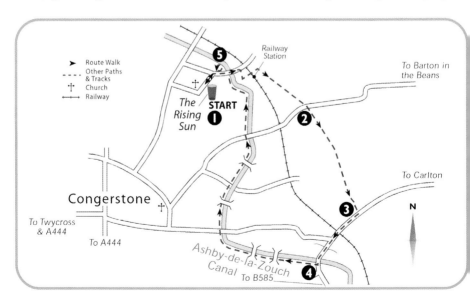

Peaceful scenery near the beginning of the walk

canal to your right. Continue beside the canal as it bends to the left. Pass under a bridge further along and keep going along the towpath. The section along here is a good place to see ducks, herons and other water birds. Pass under another bridge and continue, before passing underneath a road bridge. Over to the left is Congerstone village. Keep to the towpath and enjoy the peaceful countryside as you pass under more bridges. Further on, the towpath and canal bend sharply to the left. Pass the railway station on the opposite bank and continue.

5 Walk under bridge number 52 and then turn immediately left to arrive at a road. Turn right along the road and pass farm buildings on your left. Take the next road on your left and soon you return to the starting point at the Rising Sun.

Place of Interest

Twycross Zoo, best known for its collection of primates, is situated 3½ miles to the east of the village. Since it opened in 1963, it has grown to become one of the major British zoos. Open throughout the year. Telephone: 01872 880250.

Date walk completed:

....

Donisthorpe
The Engine Inn

This figure-of-eight route takes you through the heart of the area's rich industrial heritage. Shortly after setting off from the village of Donisthorpe, you walk along the line of a former railway (now a woodland park), which was used for transporting coal from local pits to London and the south-east. Further along the route, you pass a restored furnace, before following the route of a beautiful canal. There are also woods, brooks and ponds to explore.

The Engine Inn is over 100 years old. It has two separate bars, and a beer garden at the rear of the building. A wide variety of food is available, including jacket potatoes and sandwiches, as well as more substantial meals like steak and traditional Sunday roast. A regularly changing specials board offers yet more choice. Marston's Pedigree and Bass are always available, accompanied by various guest ales.

Opening times are 12 noon to 3 pm and 6 pm to 11 pm on Monday to Saturday, and 12 noon to 3 pm and 7 pm to 10.30 pm on Sunday. Food is available from 12 noon to 2.45 pm and 6 pm to 8.45 pm on Tuesday to Saturday, and 12 noon to 2.30 pm on Sunday (no food all day Monday or Sunday evening).

Telephone: 01530 271038.

Distance: 4¼ miles

OS Explorer 245 The National Forest, Burton upon Trent & Swadlincote GR 312138

An easy walk on largely flat ground

Starting point: The Engine Inn's car park. Please seek permission from the landlord to leave your car whilst walking.

How to get there: From Measham, which is located half a mile south of the A42, between junction 11 of the M42 and Ashby-de-la-Zouch, drive north-west on the B586. After 1¼ miles, turn left on an unclassified road to Donisthorpe. The pub can be found on your right.

The Walk

1 With the pub behind you, cross over to the opposite side of the road and then turn left along the pavement. Ignore a road off to the left and continue past the church on your right. Immediately afterwards, cross to the opposite side of the road again, and take the path on your left marked 'Ashby Woulds Heritage Trail'. Continue straight ahead on a well-surfaced path, which follows the line of the former Ashby and Nuneaton Joint Railway. It opened in 1873 and carried coal and passengers until it closed in 1981. Ignore a marked path to the right

further on, and another soon after. Cross a bridge over a stream and keep to the main path, as it curves slightly to the left. Further on, the path becomes muddy. Continue ahead until you reach a sign marked 'Moira Furnace Museum'.

2 Turn right and descend wooden steps. At the bottom of the steps, turn left. Soon after, bear round to the right. As you reach a well-surfaced path, go straight ahead and cross a playing field. Walk through a car park and pass under a height restriction, then turn right along a lane. Continue ahead to Moira Furnace Museum. Completed in 1806, this former

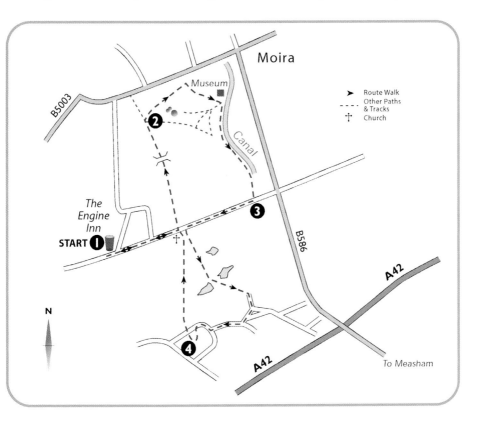

blast furnace was used to make iron until it closed in 1811, although a foundry making iron castings continued to function on the site for a further 30 years. The museum entrance is a short distance to the left. Pass the furnace on your left-hand side and then turn right along a towpath running beside the Ashby-de-la-Zouch Canal. The canal was constructed around 1800 and was used to carry coal to various cities. Pass an attractive footbridge over the canal and continue on the towpath as it curves to the left. At the end of the path, go over a stile and continue ahead. Walk through a car park until you reach a road.

❸ Turn right along the road and pass a cemetery on your right. Pass a path on your right, which was used near the start of the walk, then cross the road. Just before reaching the church, turn left along a marked path, passing the church on your right. Walk down a gentle slope and follow a left-hand fork in the path. Pass houses to your left, then go over a fence and continue, keeping a hedge to your right. Pass a pond on your left, then cross a footbridge and walk along a path between two ponds. Further on, veer slightly left, keeping a hedge to your right. On reaching a car park, walk straight ahead. Continue along a lane, then turn right along a narrow road. At a T-junction, turn right. After passing a telephone box, veer off to the right and continue along Coronation Lane.

Moira Furnace Museum is passed on the way

❹ Just before reaching a road bridge, turn left at a signed path and follow it round to the right. Turn right to pass underneath the bridge and continue along the former railway line. Keep to the main path and continue until you reach the road by the church. Turn left along the road, passing the church on your left-hand side. Keep going straight ahead and retrace your steps back to the Engine Inn.

> Date walk completed:
>
> ....

Place of Interest
Moira Furnace Museum is passed on the walk, and its interactive exhibition offers a fascinating insight into an industrial past. Open all year round. Telephone: 01283 224667.